CAMBRIDGE LIBRARY COLLECTION

Books of enduring scholarly value

History

The books reissued in this series include accounts of historical events and
movements by eye-witnesses and contemporaries, as well as landmark
studies that assembled significant source materials or developed new
historiographical methods. The series includes work in social, political and
military history on a wide range of periods and regions, giving modern
scholars ready access to influential publications of the past.

Dr Southwood Smith

Thomas Southwood Smith (1788–1861) was a minister, physician and social
reformer, who considerably improved the health of the poor by linking
sanitation with epidemics. A utilitarian, and friend of Jeremy Bentham, his
arguments in *The Use of the Dead to the Living* (1827) helped lead to the
Anatomy Act of 1832 which allowed corpses from workhouses to be sold to
medical schools, and so ended the market for grave-robbers while improving
medical education. Although the fame of his granddaughter, Octavia Hill,
has eclipsed his own reputation, Southwood Smith was an important figure
in his day, whose work initiated many public health reforms. He served
on the royal commission on children's employment, and was medical
representative on the General Board of Health to deal with the cholera
epidemic of 1848. This biography, written by his granddaughter Gertrude,
who was G. H. Lewes' daughter-in-law, was published in 1898.

T0370907

Cambridge University Press has long been a pioneer in the reissuing of out-of-print titles from its own backlist, producing digital reprints of books that are still sought after by scholars and students but could not be reprinted economically using traditional technology. The Cambridge Library Collection extends this activity to a wider range of books which are still of importance to researchers and professionals, either for the source material they contain, or as landmarks in the history of their academic discipline.

Drawing from the world-renowned collections in the Cambridge University Library, and guided by the advice of experts in each subject area, Cambridge University Press is using state-of-the-art scanning machines in its own Printing House to capture the content of each book selected for inclusion. The files are processed to give a consistently clear, crisp image, and the books finished to the high quality standard for which the Press is recognised around the world. The latest print-on-demand technology ensures that the books will remain available indefinitely, and that orders for single or multiple copies can quickly be supplied.

The Cambridge Library Collection will bring back to life books of enduring scholarly value (including out-of-copyright works originally issued by other publishers) across a wide range of disciplines in the humanities and social sciences and in science and technology.

Dr Southwood Smith

A Retrospect

GERTRUDE HILL LEWES

CAMBRIDGE
UNIVERSITY PRESS

CAMBRIDGE UNIVERSITY PRESS

Cambridge, New York, Melbourne, Madrid, Cape Town,
Singapore, São Paolo, Delhi, Tokyo, Mexico City

Published in the United States of America by Cambridge University Press, New York

www.cambridge.org
Information on this title: www.cambridge.org/9781108037983

This edition first published 1898
This digitally printed version 2011

ISBN 978-1-108-03798-3 Paperback

DR SOUTHWOOD SMITH

Swan Electric Engraving Cº

DR SOUTHWOOD SMITH

A RETROSPECT

BY

HIS GRANDDAUGHTER

MRS C. L. LEWES

WILLIAM BLACKWOOD AND SONS
EDINBURGH AND LONDON
MDCCCXCVIII

TO

MY MOTHER,

CAROLINE SOUTHWOOD HILL,

I DEDICATE THIS MEMOIR

OF

HER FATHER.

PREFACE.

IT is now nearly forty years since the death of my grandfather, Dr Southwood Smith, and with this distance of time lying between him and us, it may not be uninteresting to this generation to look back upon the origin of some of the great social reforms which have now reached such wide proportions, and to see these reforms as gathered round the life of a man who was in the forefront of the noble army which promoted them.

He, one of the first to seize a truth, one of the most indomitable to persevere in the promulgation of it when perceived, went straight forward until it prevailed, and thus became instrumental in conferring some of the widest benefits which have come to us in this century.

From his great grief in early manhood he but emerged the stronger. The force of his condensed sorrow produced an energy which carried all before it, and resulted in the strength of his middle age and the serenity of his latter years. In order that such a life—crowned by its humility —might not pass away without some permanent record of its nobleness, the following memoir has been written.

I must apologise for the frequent allusion, in the midst of grave public questions, to my own recollections ; but since all the early years of my life were passed at my grandfather's side, it has been difficult to avoid this.

Moreover, I have hoped that something picturesque and touching would be found in the relation of the strong man and little child, who worked together at various public causes, playing together in the bright intervals, and that something of the reverent enthusiasm he inspired in that child might pass, through her, to those who read these pages.

GERTRUDE LEWES.

CONTENTS.

INTRODUCTION.

CHAPTER III.

CHAPTER IV.

CHAPTER V.

CHAPTER VI.

ILLUSTRATIONS.

DR SOUTHWOOD SMITH

RECOLLECTIONS OF MY GRANDFATHER.

My first recollection of my grandfather is of him
in his study. As a little child my bed stood in
his room, and when he got up, as he used to do
in the early mornings, to write, he would take me
in his arms, still fast asleep, carry me down-stairs
to his study with him, and lay me on the sofa,
wrapped in blankets which had been arranged for
me overnight.

So when first I opened my eyes in the silent
room I saw him there, a man of some fifty years,
bending over a table covered with papers, the
light of his shaded reading-lamp shining on his
forehead and glancing down upon the papers as

A

he leant over his writing, and the firelight flickering on the other parts of the room.

The silence and the earnestness seemed wonderful and beautiful. It was strange to watch him when he did not know it. It seemed to me, then, that he had been working so through the whole night, and that some great good which I could only dimly understand was to come of it.

My lying quiet, however, did not last long, for I knew the loving merry welcome I should have when, climbing—as I hoped and believed quite unperceived—up the back of his arm-chair, I should throw myself down into his lap with a loud cry of joy, and then we should have a famous game, until either he persuaded me to go back to my blankets to await a rational hour for getting up, or sent me up-stairs to be dressed.

These two things—the intent, absorbed purpose, and the power of putting it aside to give himself up completely, with simple delight, to whatever he loved, whether to a child or to the beauty of nature — are the two that seem to me specially characteristic of him in all that later part of his life which comes within my remembrance.

Dr Southwood Smith and his grandchild Gertrude.

At this time we lived in Kentish Town, then field-surrounded, he going daily to his consulting-rooms in Finsbury Square, returning late and giving the early mornings and Sundays to public work. These hours were at that period (1840 to 1842) chiefly devoted to the question of the employment of children in coal - mines, the more deeply impressed on me because the report which he was then writing had illustrations showing the terrible condition of people working in mines.

I remember long bright Sunday mornings when he was at work endeavouring to remedy these evils. He let me do what little I could, such as the cutting out of extracts to be fastened on to the MS. report with wafers—and very particular I was as to the colour of these wafers! Sometimes all I could do to help was to be quiet—not the least hard work! Yet I loved these still Sunday mornings, and would not willingly have been shut out from them any more than from the afternoon ride which came later, when, perched up in front of him on his own horse, in the little railed saddle he had devised for me, we rode along the lanes towards Highgate. I can see now the sunset light falling on the grass and tree - stems of the Kentish Town fields as we went along.

Then came the day when the Act was brought into operation which was to regulate the employment of children in mines, and I tied blue ribbons on to his carriage horses and thought, with a child's hopefulness, that all the suffering was at once and completely over. " Then, now, they are all running over the green fields," I said.

My grandfather let me think it, and did not damp my enthusiasm by letting me know that this happy state of things was not arrived at in one day!

But although he often played merrily with me and entered into my childish joys, my grandfather was endowed with a most earnest nature and with a firmness of character which was very remarkable. He never swerved from a purpose, never vacillated. One of his sayings was, " Life is not long enough for us to reconsider our decisions."

It was probably this quiet determination, combined with his unfailing gentleness, that made him inspire so much confidence in his patients. I can fancy, in a house where illness was spreading anxiety and sorrow, the restfulness there would be in his calm presence, and I can remember the faces of those—often the very poor—who used to come up to him wishing to thank him for the life of some wife, or son, or child which they said he had saved. These things used to happen in the crowded city streets or courts, and sometimes in parts of London far away from the place where the illness had occurred. The fact that these faces were generally forgotten by him, whilst *his* was so well remembered, made a still more beautiful mystery over it. It seemed to me that there was an honour in belonging to one who was a help and support to so many. Such experiences must be familiar to those who share his profession, still I mention it as being my strong childish impression; and even now, looking back upon his life, it appears to me that he did possess, in a very high degree, not only the power of healing, but that of soothing mental suffering.

It was, in fact, this deep sympathy, joined to his remarkable insight into the relations between effects and their causes, which led him to devote

his life to the promotion of sanitary reform, when
once it had become obvious to him that all effort
to improve the condition of the people would be
impossible until its principles were known and
acted upon.

CHAPTER I.

EARLY LIFE, 1788–1820.

THOMAS SOUTHWOOD SMITH was born at Martock in Somersetshire in 1788, and was intended by his family to become a minister in the body of Calvinistic dissenters to which they belonged. He was educated with that view at the Baptist College in Bristol, where he went in 1802, being then fourteen years of age. A scholarship, entitled the "Broadmead Benefaction," was granted to him, and he held it for nearly five years.

But in the course of his earnest reading on religious subjects he was led to conclusions opposed in many ways to the doctrines he would be expected to teach; and when, in the autumn of 1807, from conscientious scruples, he felt bound to declare this to be the case, the benefaction was withdrawn. If we consider his youth and his limited means, it is clear that this avowal must have cost him no little anguish. He was at this time only eighteen. It was an early age at which to have been able to make up his mind on questions so momentous, to break away from early and dear traditions, and to face the displeasure of the Principal of the college, Dr Ryland, whom he ever revered. But honour demanded the sacrifice, and it was made.

In consequence his family cast him off at once and for ever.

During his college career, however, he had visited much at the house of Mr Read, a large manufacturer in Bristol, who was a man of noble character, and at that time one of the leading supporters of the college; and an attachment had sprung up between the young student and Mr Read's daughter Anne. This lady seems to have possessed both great personal beauty and much sweetness and strength of character; and though she in nowise changed her own religious opinions, she yet sympathised deeply with him in his earnest seeking after truth, and encouraged him to risk all—position, friends, everything—rather than act against his conscience.

Mr Read also upheld him through all his difficulties, and in the following year sanctioned their
marriage, which brought with it some few very
happy years. Two children were born—Caroline,[1]
my mother, and a year afterwards her sister
Emily.[2]

His happiness was to be but of short duration,
for in 1812 the young wife died, and left him
alone, at the age of only twenty-four, with two
little children. With what deep grief he mourned
her death his early writings show, but he met it
with a noble courage and an undiminished faith.

The course he took was a strong one. Deprived of the profession to which he had looked
forward, cut off from all intercourse with his
family, and having lost the wife he so devotedly
loved, he resolved — leaving his two children
under the gentle care of their mother's relations—
to apply himself to the study of medicine. Thus
he entered as a student at the Edinburgh University in the year 1813.

[1] Caroline Southwood Smith, married, 1835, Mr James Hill.
    Children of this marriage : Miranda Hill, Gertrude Hill
    (Mrs Charles Lewes), Octavia Hill, Emily S. Hill (Mrs
    C. E. Maurice), Florence Hill.
[2] Emily Southwood Smith, born 1810, died 1872.

At first he lived quite alone; but finding it more than he could bear, he returned to England to fetch his eldest child, then four years old.

The father and child (my mother) went from Bristol to Edinburgh in a small sailing vessel, and encountered a terrible storm, which lasted many days. She tells me that she still remembers that storm of eighty-five years ago, the thick darkness, the war of the winds, the toss of the waves, the flash of the lightning illuminating her father's face; but, most of all, she remembers the feeling of the strong arm round her, giving the sense of safety.

His interest in religious matters at this period was greater than ever; for the change in his opinions, in leading him to take a more loving view of the Divine nature, had increased his ardour for the truth, and his own personal sorrow had heightened his faith and made him wish to carry its comfort to others. As well, therefore, as pursuing his medical studies, he gathered round him in Edinburgh a little congregation for service every Sunday. The sermons preached by him then, seem to have an added depth of feeling when we know the circumstances in which they

were given; and the following words, written by
him at this time, give some insight into the calm
sublime faith which upheld him, not only then,
but throughout life.

"Can there be a more exalted pleasure," he
writes, "than that which the mind experiences
when, in moments of reflective solitude—in those
moments when it becomes tranquil and disposed
to appreciate the real value of objects—it dwells
upon the thought that there is, seated on the
throne of the universe, a Being whose eye never
slumbers nor sleeps, and who is perfect in power,
wisdom, and goodness? How little can the
storms of life assail *his* soul who rests his happiness upon this Rock of Ages! How little can
death itself appal *his* mind who feels that he is
conducted to the tomb by the hand of the
Sovereign of the universe! Yes! there is a
reality in religion; and if that happiness, which
is so often sought, and so often sought in vain—
that happiness which is worthy of a rational being,
and which at once satisfies and exalts him—be
ever tasted upon earth, it is by him who thus, in
the solitude of his heart, delights to contemplate
the idea of a presiding Benignity, the extent of

whose dominion is without limit, and the duration of whose kingdom is without end! It is a felicity which our Father sometimes sends down to the heart that is worthy of it, to give it a foretaste of its eternal portion."

Much interest was felt in the young pale student and his little girl. For all this time my mother, the little Caroline, lived with him, cheering his home-coming from the university to their rooms, and drinking in from him at a very early age—as I, her daughter, was destined to do many years after—lessons of self-devotion to great ends.

It was at this time of sorrow, and in the intervals of medical study, that he wrote his ' Illustrations of the Divine Government,' the object of which is to show how perfect is the Love that rules the world, in spite of that which seems to clash,—pain, and sorrow, and wrong— all that we call evil.

His medical studies only added to his impression of the great Whole as one perfect scheme, for he felt an intimate connection between the field of scientific research and those religious studies to which he had formerly devoted himself exclusively. This is shown in his own

words in the preface to the fourth edition of
the work, which was published in 1844.

" The contemplation," he writes, " of the
wonderful processes which constitute life, — the
exquisite mechanism (as far as that mechanism
can be traced) by which they are performed—
the surprising adjustments and harmonies by
which, in a creature like man, such diverse and
opposite actions are brought into relation with
each other and made to work in subserviency
and co-operation ; — and the divine object of
all—the communication of sensation and intelligence as the inlets and instruments of happiness — afforded the highest satisfaction to my
mind. But this beautiful world, into whose
workings my eye now searched, presented itself to my view as a demonstration that the
Creative Power is infinite in goodness, and
seemed to afford, as if from the essential ele-
ments and profoundest depths of nature, a proof
of His love."

This book came to be a help to many of all
classes and creeds, and passed through several
editions.

He was often urged to reprint it in later life,

but held it back, wishing to modify it slightly. Not that his opinion of its main principles had altered in the least degree, but that he thought he had passed too lightly over the sea of misery and crime that there is in the world ; he thought there was rather too much of the bright hopefulness of youth about it. Sorrow he had known, certainly, in the loss of his wife ; but the sorrow that comes from the loss of one who was noble and good, and who has been taken from us by death, is of quite a different kind from that which comes from a closer acquaintance with the mass of sin and misery which exists. He did not change his view that, even this, rightly understood, is consistent with the divine benevolence ; but he wished to recognise more fully its existence, and to enter more largely into the subject.

Having completed his medical studies and obtained his degree, the young physician determined to take a practice in Yeovil. The following extract from a letter, dated August 5, 1816, addressed by him to a friend in Rome,[1] shows with what views as to his future profession he quitted Scotland.

[1] The Hon. D. G. Halliburton.

" I leave Edinburgh this week," he writes ;
" I leave it with much regret, for I have found
friends here whom I shall ever remember with
respect, affection, and gratitude. I go to Yeovil, a little town in the west of England, where
it is my intention to take charge of a congregation and at the same time to practise
medicine. This double capacity of physician
to body and soul does not appear to me to be
incompatible, but how the plan will succeed can
be determined only by the test of experience.

" My expectations are not very sanguine, but
neither are my desires ambitious."

" The test of experience " proved that he was
admirably qualified for the double office he had
taken upon himself, and for some years he pursued faithfully the plan he had made.

But this quiet country life was not to be his
always. It was decreed that he should come
up to London and enter into its teeming life,
to think, and write, and labour, until he had
done his part towards lessening its mass of
misery.

CHAPTER II.

FIRST YEARS IN LONDON—DAWN OF THE SCIENCE OF MODERN HYGIENE, 1820–1834.

ON first arriving in London in 1820, my grandfather, who whilst still at Yeovil had married for the second time (Mary, daughter of Mr John Christie of Hackney),[1] settled in Trinity Square, near the Tower. He soon formed a considerable private practice, and was appointed physician to the London Fever Hospital, and he was thus led to give very special attention to the subject of fever. He also held the offices of physician to the Eastern Dispensary and to the Jews' Hospital, situated in the very heart of Whitechapel. And while his experience in the wards of the fever hospital taught him by what means that disease can most frequently be *cured*, his acquaintance with it in the homes of his East-

---

[1] *Children of this marriage:* Herman Southwood Smith, born 1819, died 1897; Spencer, Christina, both died in childhood.

end patients taught him more—how it might be *prevented.*

Almost the first writings bearing on what came to be afterwards called the "Sanitary Question" are to be found in the pages of the 'Westminster Review.' In the two first numbers of that Review, published in the year 1825, there appeared some articles on "Contagion and Sanitary Laws." These articles, published anonymously, were written by Dr Southwood Smith. It must be noted that the word "sanitary" had not then the meaning it has in these days : sanitary science was unknown, and the words "Sanitary Laws" had a no wider signification than that of the regulations of a quarantine code.

But from that time these words acquired a new meaning.

In the articles above referred to, facts were brought together which had been collected from the writings of men who had devoted years to the study of pestilences in Spain, in various ports of the Mediterranean, in Constantinople, and in the West Indies. They had gone where epidemics were raging, had risked their lives that they might increase the store of knowledge about

these fearful scourges, and might, if possible, learn
on what they depend.   Amongst these men, one
of the most distinguished was apparently a Dr
Maclean, of whom the article tells us that " when
he was in Spain in 1821 yellow fever attacked
Barcelona, and that with his wonted zeal he
hastened to the spot in order that he might fully
investigate its nature."   Dr Maclean is spoken
of as " one of those extraordinary men who is
capable of concentrating all the faculties of his
mind, and of devoting the best years of his life,
to the accomplishment of one great and benevolent object."   We are told how, " in order to
demonstrate what epidemic diseases really are,
and what they are not, and to put an end to
errors which have so long and so universally
prevailed on this subject, errors which he believes
to be the source of incalculable misery and of
certain death to millions of the human race, Dr
Maclean, with an energy scarcely to be paralleled,
has devoted thirty years—a large portion of the
active life of man.   In this cause he has re-
peatedly risked that life, and for its sake he has
encountered all sorts of suspicion and abuse." [1]

[1] Westminster Review, 1825, p. 519.

Generalising, then, from the facts which such men had collected and from others observed by himself, Dr Southwood Smith endeavours to establish the laws of epidemic disease. In the first place, he labours to prove that *epidemic* diseases are not, in the strict sense of the word, *contagious*, and that the laws which epidemic diseases observe offer a complete contrast to those which regulate contagious diseases.

" It was proved," he thought, to use his own words, " that the symptoms of epidemic diseases are not determinate and uniform. They vary in different countries and different seasons—even in the same country and the same season, and do not succeed each other in any determinate order.

" That epidemics observe certain seasons—the periods at which they commence, decline, and cease, hardly vary. For instance, the plague in Egypt begins in March or April, and ends in June or July. All epidemics in Great Britain, of which we have any record, have raged in the autumn.

" That epidemic diseases prevail most in certain countries, in certain districts, in certain towns, and in certain parts of the same town.

They prevail most in those countries which are the least cultivated; in those districts which are the most woody, the most exposed to particular winds and to inundations; in those towns which are placed in low and damp situations, and which are unprotected from certain winds; in those streets and houses, and even in those apartments of the same house, which are the most low and damp, the worst built, and the least sheltered.

" That epidemics commence, spread, and cease in a manner perfectly peculiar. They arise, for example, in some particular quarter of a town, and do not attack the other districts which happen to be nearest it in regular succession, but break out suddenly in the most distant and most opposite directions. People are attacked, *not in proportion as the inhabitants of the affected mix with the inhabitants of the unaffected places, but in proportion as the inhabitants of the unaffected expose themselves to the air of the affected places.*

" That the termination of epidemics is peculiar, since they cease suddenly at the exact period when the greatest number of persons is affected by them, and when the greatest mortality prevails. This fact is inexplicable under the supposition that epidemics owe their spread from person to person. To suppose that a disease which is propagated by contagion can rapidly decline and even suddenly cease, just when most persons are affected and the mortality is greatest—that is, when the contagious matter is proved to be in its most active and malignant state—is utterly absurd.

" That epidemics attack the same person more than once, and that relapses are frequent amongst those suffering from them, whereas contagious diseases seldom affect the same individual a second time, and relapses are most uncommon."

From all this it will be clear that the object of these articles was to prove that all epidemics have their origin in the bad sanitary conditions (as we now say) of the places in which they arise.

It happened then, as very frequently happens in all sciences when the time is ripe for a discovery, that those working in different fields of observation noticed, at the same period, the same facts—some, as for example Dr Maclean, in their posts of observation during the epidemics in distant countries; Dr Southwood Smith in the fever-

haunts of London.   But it remained for him,
collecting together all the experience and generalising from it, to announce the law on which
they depend.

Those who thus arrived at the great principle
of the connection between defective sanitary conditions and disease, laid the foundation of Sanitary Reform.   That connection is an old truth
now,—one of those about which it is difficult
to realise that it could ever have been unknown
to the world ; but in those days it was unknown
and unrecognised, and amongst the few who
began to recognise it, there were scarcely any
who saw to what wide practical results such
truths ought to lead.

My grandfather, however, saw that if the principle were once established, not only would the
quarantine laws, at that time absurd and ineffi-
cacious, be modified ; not only would our merchant ships be released from spending long
weary months in unhealthy ports, while their
crews were perhaps contracting, from their con-
finement, the very diseases which they were
supposed to have brought with them from foreign
lands ; not only would the poor sufferers from

plague and yellow fever cease to be imprisoned
in the poisoned districts whose air had just given
them the pestilence;—not only would these *false*
precautions cease, but the true ones would be
taken : the *causes* of disease would be removed ;
and thus, wherever a knowledge of this law
spread and was acted on, disease and death
would diminish.

Might not, he thought, something practical
be done *now* and *here* if these facts were once
generally known ?   Epidemics throughout follow
the same laws.   Were not the very causes which
produce plague in Egypt operating now to produce
typhus fever in Bethnal Green and Whitechapel ?
We might not be able to stop the pestilential,
moisture - laden wind that came down to Cairo
each year at the time of the inundation of the
Nile, but could we not do something towards
purifying that which crept into the rooms of our
own poor from undrained courts and stagnant
pools ?   Could we not, if people once believed
and acted on their belief, banish the yearly
epidemic fever from the back - streets of our
large towns ?

Dr Southwood Smith believed that this great

result would follow from the general acceptance of the truth of the principle he had announced. He gave his life to spreading the knowledge of it.

By the articles in the 'Westminster Review' something was done towards enlightening the public mind, for I find that they attracted the attention of leading men in and out of Parliament, and were often referred to in the debates in both Houses.

Five years more of daily experience and constant thought passed before his 'Treatise on Fever' was published.[1] It entered fully into all the phenomena of the disease and into the question of its treatment. It added largely to the knowledge of fever existing at that time, and was welcomed by the medical profession. 'The Medico-Chirurgical Review,' the highest authority of that day, pronounced it to be "the best work on Fever that ever flowed from the pen of physician in any age or country." It was for a long time the standard work on the subject with which it dealt. The most important part of the work, however, as might be expected, is that which relates, not to the treatment of disease

[1] Longmans, 1830.

(which has since his time much changed) but
to its *causes*. And here we find an elaboration of
the principles laid down five years before in his
articles in the 'Westminster Review.' Those
articles had been the result of a rapid glance
which had gone to the very root of things,
though when they were written their writer had
held his position at the Fever Hospital for one
year only, and had therefore not acquired the
large experience of fever which he subsequently
attained. But the five years that had passed
since they were written could not change —
could only strengthen — his conviction of the
truth of the principles which he had previously
expounded.

In the 'Treatise on Fever,' as in the articles
just quoted, it is enforced upon us, that since
epidemics are everywhere the same, when they
reach our own country we must expect to find
conditions similar to those which produce pestilence in foreign countries. He writes as follows :—

  "*The room of a fever patient, in a small and
heated apartment of London, with no perflation of
fresh air, is perfectly analogous to a stagnant pool*

in Ethiopia full of the bodies of dead locusts. The poison generated in both cases is the same ; the difference is merely in the degree of its potency. Nature with her burning sun, her stilled and pent-up wind, her stagnant and teeming marsh, manufactures plague on a large and fearful scale. Poverty in her hut, covered with her rags, surrounded by her filth, striving with all her might to keep out the pure air and to increase the heat, imitates Nature but too successfully ; the process and the product are the same, the only difference is in the magnitude of the result. Penury and ignorance can thus, at any time and in any place, create a mortal plague." [1]

Dr Southwood Smith has been accused of ignoring the fact that those suffering from fever can communicate the disease to others—of "infection," as it is called. But he did not. He shows, on the contrary, that the atmosphere of a room such as that spoken of in the passage just quoted must have the power of inducing fever in others besides the patient. He even says that "the poison formed by the exhalations given off from the living bodies of those affected by fever is by

---

[1] Treatise on Fever, p. 324.

far the most potent febrile poison derived from animal origin."

Then, it might be asked, of what consequence is it to insist on the disease being non-contagious? If fever-patients can give fever to others, it is a mere matter of words whether you choose to call it "contagious" or "infectious."

It is, however, of the utmost consequence to fix the attention on the difference ; because, if that is done, the real seat of the danger will be clearly seen, and those whose duty it is to enter the rooms of the sick will know that their danger rarely lies in touching the patient, and may be prevented by abundance of fresh air and scrupulous cleanliness.

In order to emphasise this side of the truth my grandfather wrote as follows (and, though it may seem to require qualification, the *general* truth of his remark will be admitted by all) : " No fever produced by contamination of the air can be communicated to others in a pure air — there never was an instance of such communication."

The form of poison given off from a fever patient is, besides, not so much to be feared as other forms of that poison, because, though it is potent, it has not a wide range; when let out into the fresh air, it is so far diluted that its power is reduced to a minimum.

An epidemic, he asserts, can only arise from some cause sufficient to affect a whole district. Continually we are brought back to observe this universal cause of fevers; to see that, whether in the sudden falling off of an army to half its numbers, or in the prostration of a whole ship's crew on approaching shore, or in the plague devastating Cairo, this one source may be traced as the true one. Bad air comes from the marsh near which the army is stationed; bad air, poisoned by decaying vegetation, comes off shore to the ship; bad air enters the houses of Cairo. We are shown that Cairo is the birthplace of the plague, because it is a city crowded with a poor population; because it is built with close and narrow streets; because it is situated in the midst of a sandy plain at the foot of a mountain, which keeps off the wind, and is therefore exposed to stifling heat; and, above all, because it has a great canal which, though filled with water at the inundation of the Nile, becomes dry as the river gets lower, and thus emits an intolerable smell from the mud and from the offensive matter that is thrown into it.

Besides being thus shown that, in all places in which epidemics appear, some sanitary defect may be found, we are shown that they come back and back to the same places, and that, if these defects are removed, the epidemics will not return. So we are led on to the great idea that they are *preventible*.

The facts advanced to prove these principles have not, of course, the wide range, the distinct statistical exactness, of those which the further progress of sanitary science has now enabled people to bring forward ; but it is very interesting to see how all further advance has been but a development of the principles brought forward in this 'Treatise on Fever,' just as it was itself but a development of those brought forward five years before. Hardly any investigations had yet been made, but the results which research would bring to light are here foreshadowed. Even the direction which such research would take is indicated, for we are told, at the end of the chapter which treats of the "Causes of Fever," that—

" Further inquiries are necessary — such as, whether the vegetable and animal poisons we have been considering be the *only* true, exciting cause of fever ;[1] by what means its general diffusion is effected ; on what conditions its propagation depends ; by what measures its extension may be checked and its power diminished or destroyed ; what circumstances in the modes of life, in the habits of society, in the structure of houses, in the condition of the public streets and common sewers, in the state of the soil over large districts of the country as influenced by the mode of agriculture, drainage, and so on, favour or check the origin and propagation of this great curse of civilised, no less than of uncivilised, man."

Not a mere article or book contained the result of such inquiries. They occupied the greater part of his life, and that of many others. Their outcome is the present state of sanitary knowledge.

If some people think there was nothing new in the view of epidemics insisted on in this

[1] Modern investigations have proved, for instance, that contaminated water or milk will produce an epidemic as well as contaminated *air*. But all these poisons arise from bad sanitary conditions.—G. L.

Treatise, they have only to see what was the common opinion at that time amongst medical men. A few shared the writer's opinions, but the majority of English physicians then certainly took quite the opposite view. When Asiatic cholera first broke out in 1831, it was of no avail that the physicians of Bengal had declared unanimously that "the attempt to prevent the introduction of cholera by a rigorous quarantine had always and utterly failed"; it was of no avail that the articles on "Quarantine Laws" had, six years before, urged the same truth; the London College of Physicians issued, notwithstanding, a notification that, wherever cholera appeared, the sick should be collected together in houses, which should be marked conspicuously *Sick ;* and that, even after the sufferers had been removed, and the houses purified, *Caution* should be marked on them. That the dead from cholera should be buried in separate ground ; that food to be delivered at a house where any one was sick should be placed outside, and only taken in when the person who brought it had gone away ; and that no one who had communicated

with a cholera patient should, during twenty
days after, communicate with the healthy.

If cholera resisted all these precautions, and
became fatal in the terrific way it had done in
other countries, the authorities announced "that
it might become necessary to draw a strong body
of troops or police round the affected places."

This proclamation of the physicians of 1831
was published throughout the land in the form
of an Order of the King in Council. It might
have been more to the purpose to have cleansed
the affected town.

" But," says Mr Howell,[1] " the strong good
sense of the public averted many of the mis-
chiefs which these scientific advisers would
have produced had their counsels been carried
into execution. The preventive measures, which
were eventually adopted by them, consisted in
prohibiting intercourse between one town and
another by sea, and permitting it by land : thus
communication between London and Edinburgh
by stage - coach was perfectly free and unin-
terrupted, while communication between those
capitals by sea was prohibited with such rigour

[1] Origin and Progress of Sanitary Reform. T. Jones Howell.

that no interest, however powerful, could procure an exemption! Francis Jeffrey — at this time holding the high office of Lord Advocate of Scotland, and whose influence from his personal and official connections was very great — was unable to obtain permission for his faithful servant, in the last stage of dropsy, to go from London to Leith by water, lest he should carry with him to his native country by that mode of conveyance, not the dropsy which he had, but the cholera which he had not.

" ' You will be sorry,' writes Jeffrey to Miss Cockburn, ' to hear that poor old Fergus is so ill that I fear he will die very soon. I have made great efforts to get him shipped off to Scotland, where he wishes much to go ; but the *quarantine regulations are so absurdly severe that, in spite of all my influence with the Privy Council, I have not been able to get a passage for him, and he is quite unable to travel by land.* . . . He has decided water in the chest and swelling in all his limbs. The doctors say he may die any day, and that it is scarcely possible he can recover.' " [1]

[1] Cockburn's Life of Jeffrey, ii. 247.

Mr Howell adds that these examples are not adduced for the purpose of casting obloquy on the eminent physicians of that day, who vainly endeavoured to reduce to practice in the nineteenth century the standard, but obsolete, doctrines taught almost universally in the medical schools, but solely for the purpose of displaying the state of the science of Public Health in the year 1831-32, as far as the physicians of highest reputation and largest practice may be taken as its exponents.

It need hardly be said that it is with this purpose only that these facts are again cited here.

CHAPTER III.

LONDON CONTINUED—LITERARY AND OTHER WORK, 1820–1834.

THE 'Treatise on Fever' held an important place in the development of that sanitary ideal to the realisation of which my grandfather afterwards devoted himself almost exclusively; but in the course of the years which are treated of in this chapter, he wrote much on other subjects.

During this time severe money losses had necessitated the breaking up of the establishment in Trinity Square; retrenchment became a duty; Mrs Southwood Smith went abroad with the three children of the second marriage[1] to carry on their education; and (his two elder daughters, Caroline and Emily, being engaged

[1] Herman Southwood, born 1820, died 1897; Christina and Spencer, died in childhood.

in teaching away from home) my grandfather once more retired to a strictly studious and professional life at his consulting-rooms in New Broad Street, giving much time to literary work, including the writing of a large number of physiological articles for the ' Penny Encyclopædia.'

Dr Southwood Smith at this period assisted in founding the ' Westminster Review.' This Review, supported as it was by men of great ability and earnest thought, took, as is well known, a leading place in the promotion of the political and social reforms of the day.

His own contributions to it were many. Besides the articles on " Quarantine and Sanitary Laws " already mentioned, the one on " Education," which appeared in the first number, may be specially referred to.

There was also one calling attention to the horrors arising from there being no proper provision for supplying the anatomical schools with the means of dissection, which led to very practical results.

" Body-snatching " is now an extinct crime. Such was the name given· to the practice of robbing graves of the bodies of the dead in order to sell them for the purpose of dissection. Such practices were an outrage against all the feelings which render the resting - places of the dead hallowed spots. One can imagine the horror which the friends of the newly interred must have experienced in finding that their graves had been violated during the night; and worse still were the midnight scenes when the work was interrupted by the police, and struggles ensued.

The men who carried on this trade were called " resurrection-men " : they were a depraved and dangerous class, and if the state of things then existing had caused no other evil than that of educating such a class, it would still have been worth much effort to get it remedied.

Without bodies for dissection medical education was impossible, and at that time there was only one legal means by which they could be obtained : those of executed criminals were made over to the medical profession for the purpose of dissection. But this source was, happily, even then a scanty one. Until, therefore, some other provision was made, the employment of " resurrection-men," though against the law, and in itself revolting to the professors of anatomy, was a necessity.

The difficulty was an increasing one. The wretched men whose trade it was to supply the medical schools were punished with imprisonment and heavy fines, and were, not unnaturally, regarded with abhorrence by the mob—such abhorrence that it was often difficult to protect them from its fury when arrested. In Scotland, especially, this popular feeling was so strong that disgraceful outrages were committed against those even *suspected* of being concerned in exhumation ; the churchyards were watched, and the obstacles in obtaining subjects for the schools had become so many that the students were fast deserting them. Indeed throughout Great Britain it appeared as if there would soon be a general desertion of all the native schools, and that students would go to Paris for the education they could not get at home.

In the article by Dr Southwood Smith which first called public attention to these evils, he points out, in a very striking manner, the paramount necessity of a supply of subjects. He reminds his readers of the wild theories of former

times when anatomical knowledge was not possessed, and enforces on their attention the fact
that this knowledge can only be acquired, with
any degree of perfection, by means of dissection.
He further reminds them that no operation can
be performed without torture to the living, and
danger to life itself, by the hand of a surgeon
unpractised in dissection ; and no clear judgment
formed by the physician on the diseases of the
human frame—diseases generally seated in organs
hidden from the eye—without a study of the
internal structure.

After shortly passing over the evils of the
system then prevailing, which have just been
pointed out—evils which were then very generally known—he suggests the remedy,—a very
simple one. It was, to cease to give the bodies
of executed criminals for anatomical purposes,
and thus in a measure to take off the stigma
on dissection ; and then to appropriate to that
purpose the bodies of all those who die in hospitals and workhouses *unclaimed by relatives.*

Nothing was done for some time, till in 1828,
three years after this paper was written, there
came the horrible discovery that the difficulty

of obtaining subjects from the churchyards had become so great that two men, Burke and Hare, had resorted to murder to supply the need—the temptation having been the large price to be obtained for bodies.

When things had come to this climax, legislalative attention was aroused. At this time the article which had appeared in the 'Westminster Review' was reprinted as a pamphlet, under the title of 'The Use of the Dead to the Living.' In this form it went through several editions, a copy being presented to members of both Houses of Parliament.

The measures recommended in it were mainly adopted by the Legislature, and have proved completely successful.

There is something at first sight sad in a plan which lets anything that is painful in the thought of such an appropriation of the bodies of the dead fall exclusively on the poor. This did not fail to suggest itself to my grandfather's mind. But it is to the survivors alone that such pain comes, and these friendless ones would have none left to shrink from this use of their remains. Such were to be chosen for the necessary purpose, not because they were "poor," but because they were "unclaimed." Neither was any pain arising from this arrangement to be compared with that springing from the forcible seizure of bodies in the old times. Out of *that* arose, necessarily, scenes of horror revolting to all sense of the respect due to the dead ; while their quiet removal from the hospital to the anatomical school, to be followed, after the necessary dissection, by their burial, is widely different. It seemed, moreover, that the interest of the poor specially demanded a widespread anatomical knowledge in medical men, since they, more than all others, suffered when the means of gaining it were limited. " Poverty, it is true," my grandfather writes, " is a misfortune ; poverty, it is true, has terror and pain enough in itself. No legislature ought by any act to increase its wretchedness ; but the measure here proposed is pregnant with good to the poor, and would tend, more than can be estimated, to lessen the misery of their condition. For it would give knowledge to the lowest practitioners of the medical art—that is, to persons who are at present lamentably deficient, and into whose hands the great bulk of the poor fall. And, after all, the true question is, whether the surgeon shall be allowed to gain knowledge by operating on the bodies of the dead, or driven to obtain it by practising on the bodies of the living. If the dead bodies of the poor are not appropriated to this use, their living bodies must be, and will be. The rich will always have it in their power to select, for the performance of an operation, the surgeon who has signalised himself by success; but that surgeon, if he has not obtained the dexterity which ensures success by dissecting and operating on the bodies of the dead, must have acquired it by making them on the living bodies of the poor."

It was said at the time by objectors that the measure in question would deter patients from entering the hospitals, and add terrors to workhouses, but experience has proved that my grandfather was right : the adoption of his plan has not been found to have the slightest effect of the kind.

In considering the work of this period of my grandfather's life, I ought not to omit to mention his lectures, which were full of the same earnestness and originality that characterised all he did. He was lecturer at the Webb Street School of Anatomy, where he gave a course on "Forensic

Medicine," which made much impression at the time. He gave also courses of popular lectures on physiology at the London Institution and elsewhere. To those at the London Institution ladies were admitted—a permission unusual in those times.

One lecture, delivered on a very remarkable occasion, must be mentioned here. My grandfather was the friend and physician of Jeremy Bentham, and was called upon, after his death, to perform a duty which he had solemnly undertaken. The venerable philosopher died in 1832 at the age of eighty-five, and by will desired that his body should be used for the purposes of dissection. He intrusted to Dr Southwood Smith, in conjunction with two other friends, the task of seeing this disposition properly fulfilled, trusting that they would not be deterred by opposition or obloquy.

This disposition of his body was not a recent act. By a will, dated as far back as 1769, it was left, for the same purpose, to his friend Dr Fordyce. The reason at that time assigned for this is expressed by Bentham in the following remarkable words :—

"This my will and special request I make, not out of affectation of singularity, but to the intent and with the desire that mankind may reap some small benefit by my decease, having hitherto had small opportunities to contribute thereto while living."

By a memorandum affixed to this document it is clear that it had undergone revision as lately as two months before his death, and that this part of it, originally made when he was twenty-one, was again deliberately and solemnly confirmed by him at eighty-five.

In thus appropriating his remains to the service of mankind, Bentham carried out, to the last moment of his life, and even after his death, his principle of "Utility."

The subject of dissection was agitating the public mind : the "Anatomy Bill" was not yet passed, and the idea might well present itself to a benevolent mind such as his, that to show a thorough absence of horror or dislike to the idea of being dissected after death would be a means of lessening the prejudice which existed against it.

Whatever may be thought of the "greatest happiness principle" of this philosopher, it did not cause him to lead a selfish or epicurean life. The long calm expanse of eighty - five years was filled with simple pleasures, with hard work, and contained many sacrifices to the cause of truth.

My grandfather bears his testimony to the wonderful energy and self-devotion of Bentham during his life in these words :—

" Bentham's object was no less a one than to construct an all-comprehensive system of morals and an all-comprehensive code of laws. For the accomplishment of a work so prodigious he put forth an energy commensurate to the end. The extent of mental labour required for this undertaking, and actually brought to it, is truly extraordinary. Every day for nearly half a century did he devote to it never less than eight hours, often ten, and sometimes twelve."

And now, when this busy life was stilled, my grandfather was bound to carry out as fully as possible Bentham's wish that in death too he might be useful. He delivered the oration over the body, in the Webb Street School of Anatomy, on the evening of the 9th of June 1832. One who was there thus writes of it :—

"None who were present can ever forget that impressive scene. The room is small and circular, with no windows, but a central skylight, and was filled, with the exception of a class of medical students and some eminent members of that profession, by friends, disciples, and admirers of the deceased philosopher, comprising many men celebrated for literary talent, scientific research, and political activity. The corpse was on the table in the centre of the room, directly under the light, clothed in a night-dress, with only the head and hands exposed. There was no rigidity in the features, but an expression of placid dignity and benevolence. This was at times rendered almost vital by the reflection of the lightning playing over them ; for a storm arose just as the lecturer commenced, and the profound silence in which he was listened to was broken, and only broken, by loud peals of thunder, which continued to roll at intervals throughout the delivery of his most appropriate and often affecting address. With the feelings which touch the heart in the contemplation of departed greatness, and in the presence of death, there mingled a sense of the power which that

lifeless body seemed to be exercising in the con-
quest of prejudice for the public good, thus co-
operating with the triumphs of the spirit by
which it had been animated. It was a worthy
close of the personal career of the great philosopher and philanthropist. Never did corpse of
hero on the battle-field, with his martial cloak
around him, or funeral obsequies chanted by
stoled and mitred priests in Gothic aisles, excite
such emotions as the stern simplicity of that
hour in which the principle of utility triumphed
over the imagination and the heart."

In the year 1834 my grandfather published
his book entitled 'The Philosophy of Health,'[1]
the preparation of which had been a work of
great care, and had occupied much time for
several years before. This book, which was,
perhaps, the first attempt to bring the truths
of human physiology within the comprehension
of the general reader, achieved a marked success. It was full of the clearness and force
which characterised all the writings of its author.
The strides of modern science have now, of
course, left its physiological teaching far behind,

---

[1] Longmans, 1834.

but at the time it did original educational work and added lustre to his name.

His life in chambers must have been an arduous one—first at 36 New Broad Street, afterwards at 38 Finsbury Square,—his days given up to his ever-increasing practice, his mornings and evenings to writing : the amount achieved was prodigious, and he allowed himself but little relaxation.

I may mention that it was at this time that my grandfather first visited at the house of old Mr Gillies, a city merchant of refined literary tastes and the father of the two distinguished women, Mary and Margaret Gillies (author and artist), who afterwards became the friends for life of himself, his wife, and daughters, and in whose home he—and I with him—had rooms in Kentish Town and afterwards at Highgate, though he occupied for professional purposes the rooms in the city to which I have before referred.

CHAPTER IV.

WORK ON THE FACTORY COMMISSION, 1833.

IN the year 1833 it became clear that some legal interference was necessary with regard to Factories.

In order to understand the abuses which existed in factories in 1833, we must revert to the system of employment at the end of the last century and trace its gradual development. At that period all the spinning and weaving of the country was domestic, the spinning being carried on in farmhouses and scattered cottages in rural places by the mothers and daughters of the families, and the weaving by men working in their own homes in towns and villages. This peaceful state of things did not last beyond the beginning of the present century. The " spinning-jenny " and " power-loom " were invented,

and changes occurred. Large buildings were
now needed to carry on the work, and mills
and factories sprang up beside the streams of
Nottinghamshire, Derbyshire, and Lancashire,
these places being chosen because water was
required to turn the new machinery. The
water-wheel now did much of the work which
had formerly needed the strong arms of men,
but the small and nimble fingers of children
were henceforth called into play, as they were
found to be specially fitted for much of that
which remained to be done by hand. Thus
it came about that children's labour, in consequence of its greater cheapness, was substi-
tuted for that of grown people.

In order to get a sufficient supply of children, which the scanty population near the mills
could not afford, manufacturers applied to the
managers of the workhouses in London and
other large towns, for pauper children to be taken
as apprentices. Hundreds, it is said even thousands, of children were thus taken away from
even the slight protection which the tender
mercies of the workhouse authorities of that
day might afford, and placed entirely in the

power of the master manufacturer, or, worse
still, of his overseer.

The evils that resulted from this apprenticeship system resembled those springing from
slavery. One writer [1] says :—

" There is abundant evidence on record, and
preserved in the recollection of some who still
live, to show that, in many of the manufacturing districts, cruelties the most heartrending
were practised upon the unoffending and friendless creatures who were thus consigned to the
care of the master manufacturers; that they
were harassed to the brink of death by excess
of labour, that they were flogged, fettered, and
tortured to the most exquisite refinements of
cruelty; that they were in many cases starved
to the bone whilst flogged to their work; and
that, in some instances, they were driven to
commit suicide to evade the cruelties of a world
where, though born into it so recently, their
happiest moments had been passed in the garb
and in the coercion of a workhouse. The
beautiful and romantic valleys of Derbyshire,
Lancashire, and Nottinghamshire, secluded from

---

[1] M. Fielden, M.P., ' The Curse of the Factory System.'

the public eye, became the dismal solitudes of
torture and of many a murder."

The Legislature interfered, and in 1802 passed
an Act for regulating factories and protecting
the apprentices employed in them. This Act
was brought in and carried by Sir Robert Peel,
the father of the statesman who repealed the
Corn Laws, and himself a large manufacturer.

A further change in the history of manufacture, however, occurred. The steam - engine
was invented, and when its power was applied
to manufacture, it was no longer necessary to
build factories where water-power was at hand ;
they were henceforth principally established in
towns. Apprentices were now but little employed ; free, paid child-labour, here to be obtained in abundance, was preferred by the millowners. They had never wished for apprentices ;
the charge of them had always entailed considerable trouble ; the responsibility was felt
heavily by conscientious masters, whilst the legal
restrictions of Sir Robert Peel's Act prevented
the avaricious and hard-hearted from profiting
by the abuses of the system. Apprenticeship
therefore died a natural death.

It might be thought that children employed under the new plan, receiving wages and living at home under the protection of their parents, would suffer no hardships calling for legal restraint; but representations having been made to the Government that abuses had crept in, a Royal Commission of inquiry was determined upon in 1833.

On this occasion Dr Southwood Smith was appointed by the Government a member of this Commission, conjointly with Mr Tooke and Mr Edwin Chadwick.[1]

Their first work was to send district commissioners into the manufacturing regions to collect evidence, and the results of those inquiries were embodied in the general Report. My grandfather took a deep interest in the subject, for the evils disclosed by the inspection, if not so great as they had been under the apprenticeship system, were still sufficiently appalling : children, some of them not more than five years old, were obliged to work the same number of

[1] This Commission, for considering the employment of children in *factories*, preceded by eleven years the one relating to their employment in *mines* alluded to in the Introduction.

hours as the adult operatives—twelve, fourteen,
or sixteen hours a - day — sometimes the whole
night; their health was thus often ruined for
life; neither time nor strength remained for education; they were growing up totally ignorant;
and they were, besides, often unkindly treated.

It is sad to see in the Report such words
as these, quoted from the children's lips : " I
am sick tired, especially in the winter nights."
" So tired when I leave the mill that I can
do nothing." " I feel so tired when I gang
home that I throw myself down, no caring what
I does." " So tired I am not able to set one
foot by the other." " Many a time I have been
so fatigued I could hardly take off my clothes
at night, or put them on in the morning. My
mother would be raging at me, because when
I sat down I could not get up again through
the house."

As to their ruined health, such sentences as
these foretell it : " Many nights I do not get
a wink of sleep from the pain." " My knees
failed from the work." Or, " Severe pains would
come on, particularly in the morning."

The evidence of the overseers and managers

is scarcely less strong than that of the little sufferers themselves.

One manager says : " I have known the children hide themselves in the wool so that they could not go home when the work was over. I have seen six or eight fetched out of the stove and beat out of the mill."

Another says : " After the children from eight to twelve years old had worked eight or nine hours, they were nearly ready to faint : only kept to their work by being spoken to, or by a little chastisement to make them jump up. I was sometimes obliged to chastise them when they were almost fainting, and it hurt my feelings ; then they would spring up and work pretty well for another hour ; but the last two or three hours were my hardest work, for they then got so exhausted."

And a third manager says : " I have seen them fall asleep, and they were performing their work with their hands, while they were asleep, after the 'billy' had stopped and their work was over."

Two great objections were made to any legislative limitation of the number of hours of chil-

dren's labour. One was, that it was impossible
to shorten their hours of work without also short-
ening those of the adults, who could not go
on without them ; the other, that it was wrong
to restrict the liberty of the subject.

The first of these was, truly, a difficulty ; but
if the evil was so very great, it appeared to
my grandfather and those acting with him that
some change *must* be made in the mode of
working, rather than overtax the children to
this extent. Relays of children must be obtained, or grown - up workers must be substi-
tuted as assistants.

With regard to the second objection—that it
would be restricting the liberty of private indi-
viduals if the law interfered—the Report shows
that children, at the age at which they suffered
these injuries, were not free agents, but were
let out to hire by their parents, by whom their
wages were appropriated, and who were easily
rendered callous to their children's wrongs by
a threat of dismissal, or a bribe of an additional
penny an hour of wage. If the law did not
step in to protect these unfortunate little ones
from parents whose selfishness and ignorance

was allowing them to grow up diseased and benighted, where, argues the Report, was their help to come from ?

The question as to whether it is right in any instance for the Government to intervene between parent and child, is now practically settled by the many laws and enactments which regulate children's education and hours of labour. But in those days the idea of any restriction of a parent's right over his child excited much opposition. It was regarded by many people as both impracticable and undesirable.

The reformers, however, carried their point and achieved success. That very year the Factory Act passed, and the recommendations of the Report were nearly all embodied in it. No child was allowed to be employed at all under eight years old; children between eight and thirteen were only allowed to work six and a half hours a-day; and all those employed were obliged to attend school for three hours a-day. Inspectors were appointed to see that the provisions of the Act were fully carried out.

Of course there was considerable indignation on the part of the millowners, but many of those who at first objected to the restrictions were afterwards convinced of their utility, and as time passed on this conviction spread amongst all classes and gathered strength.

The only modifications of the Act of 1833 which have been made since, have been mere extensions of its principles. The regulations, which at first applied to cotton, cloth, and silk mills only, have been extended by subsequent Acts to bleaching and dyeing works. Powers have also been given to compel the fencing of machinery, and to enforce other safeguards against injury to the workpeople.

Even after the Factory Commission had finished its work, and had ceased to exist, my grandfather continued to watch with interest the results of what had been done. Five years afterwards, the House of Commons having ordered a Return showing the working of the educational provisions of the Act, he went down himself to various mills, and I find his copy of the Return thickly pencilled with marginal notes like the following :—

" I visited this mill myself with a view to examine the school." " The whole neighbourhood was opposed to the direction of the mill. They now consider it a great blessing." " The children of the higher class of people are anxious to get employment in the mills."

It must have given him great delight to feel that, as was said by a writer eleven years later—

" The present Act has led to an amelioration of the treatment, and an improvement in the physical and moral character, of the vast juvenile population, such as was never before effected by an Act of Parliament; while the benefits resulting from it to all parties, the employers no less than the employed, are not only rapidly multiplying and extending, but are becoming more and more the subjects of general acknowledgment and gratulation. There is reason to believe that the total number employed in factory labour in the United Kingdom is little short of 1,000,000.[1] In one district, not by any means one of the largest, the number of children attending school was increased from 200 to 2316."

[1] This was in 1844.

CHAPTER V.

RISE OF THE SANITARY MOVEMENT, 1837.

PERHAPS the most necessary and the most tried quality in a reformer is Patience. Notwithstanding the publication of the 'Treatise on Fever' in 1830, and the tribute paid by the scientific world to its masterly exposition of the treatment and causes of the disease, notwithstanding the constant and ardent endeavours of the author to propagate his views, yet seven long years passed away before he was able to awaken the apathy of the public and the authorities.

Year after year went by, and the wards of the Fever Hospital continued to be supplied from the same districts, from the same courts and lanes—even from the very same house—as before. The preventible suffering, thus daily brought before my grandfather's eyes, was a daily reminder of the urgent need for help—of the necessity for taking practical steps to diminish it.

In 1837 the opportunity came for pressing forward in the cause. That year a frightful epidemic fever broke out in London, arousing general alarm, and demanding special inquiry. The pressure on the poor-rates became excessive, and my grandfather was appointed by the Poor Law Commissioners to report on the eastern districts of London, Drs Arnott and Kay being appointed to other districts.

The title of the Report presented by him is at once striking. He called it, " Report on the Physical Causes of Sickness and Mortality to which the Poor are particularly exposed, *and which are capable of prevention by Sanitary Measures.*" Its opening words are,—

"Some of the severest evils at present incident to the condition of poverty, which have a large share in inducing its high rate of sickness and mortality, are the consequences of improvidence. Such evils are capable of being remedied only by bringing the poor under the influence of the inducements to forethought and prudence.

" But there are evils of another class, more
general and powerful in their operation, which
can be avoided by no prudence, and removed
by no exertion, on the part of the poor. Among
the gravest, and at the same time the most
remediable, of these latter evils, is the exposure
to certain noxious agents generated and accumu-
lated in the localities in which the poor are
obliged to take up their abode, and to the per-
nicious influence of which they are constantly,
and for the most part unconsciously, subjected.

" It is the object of the present Report to
direct attention to the nature and extent of this
evil, and to show how important it is that its
mitigation, and, as far as may be found practicable, its entire removal, should form a part
of every exertion that is made for improving
the physical condition of the poor."

These words would seem to strike the key-
note of Sanitary Reform.

In order to make the Report more full and
impressive, Dr Southwood Smith writes an exact
account of what he saw. He went personally
over the greater part of the Bethnal Green
and Whitechapel districts. " I traversed," he

says, "a circle of from six to seven miles in extent. I wrote the account of the places I am about to notice on the spot; I entered many of the houses and examined their condition as to cleanliness, ventilation, as well as the state of the people themselves, who were at the time labouring under fever."

The descriptions that follow are too dreadful to be dwelt upon in detail here. We are shown individually the houses of Whitechapel : they are piled storey above storey, and are teeming with people; the streets, courts, and alleys are so built that all current of air is blocked out, and no measures whatever are taken to secure cleanliness. We are shown Bethnal Green, flat, low, damp, wasted. Here the houses are not so closely packed—there are open spaces ; but these are for the most part undrained marshes, and the air coming across them is poisonous rather than life-giving. Straggling rows of rickety cottages look out upon stagnant swamps ; their miserable gardens are scattered over with uncleared dust and refuse of all kinds, and are surrounded with black and overflowing ditches, to cross which you must pass over rotting planks used as bridges : there are houses which contain only two rooms, the larger being 9 feet by 7 and 7 feet high, the smaller not able to contain an ordinary-sized bed.

If the house has more rooms, it probably contains many families, and a state of overcrowding is produced nearly as fatal as that which prevails in the parts of London where the houses stand more thickly.

The picture comes vividly before us of the dismal homes, with their melancholy gardens where the pale children play by the black ditches; their green damp walls; the rags stuffed into the broken windows to keep out the tainted outside air; and the crowds huddled together breathing the suffocating air within doors. It is easy to realise the hopeless efforts of the poor inhabitants to fight against the dirt and disease which all those efforts are powerless to overcome!

No wonder then, that, in the words of his Report, we are told that "in many parts of both these districts fever of a malignant kind and fatal character is always more or less prevalent; that in some streets it has recently prevailed in *almost every house;* in some in *every house;* and, in some few instances, in *every room of every house.* Cases are recorded in which every member of a family has been attacked in succession, of whom, in every such case, several have died : some whole families have been swept away. Instances are detailed in which there have been found, in one small room, six persons lying ill of fever together : I have myself seen this—four in one bed and two in another."

He once more enforces the preventibleness of this dreadful state of things—how entirely it was within the power of man to change it by wise attention to the laws of health. He points out parts of the districts which had always remained comparatively healthy, and some, formerly haunts of fever, where during the last epidemic no single case had occurred, owing to sanitary improvements.

The necessity for providing in some way for the airing of streets and courts in densely populated neighbourhoods, by the knocking down of houses or other expedients, is insisted upon. Its difficulty is admitted, but still it is urged.

E

"Though it might seem a hopeless task," he says, "to set about ventilating such districts as Bethnal Green and Whitechapel, yet, if the importance of the principle be duly appreciated and the object be kept steadily in view, much may be accomplished. In some of the worst localities in these districts, at moderate expense, means might be taken to introduce free currents of air, where at present the air is perfectly stagnant and stifling. Some of the improvements recently made in the City of London show to what extent it is possible to introduce good ventilation into the heart of the most densely populated part of the Metropolis."

In this Report my grandfather also draws attention to the state of the Workhouses. He was writing to the Poor Law Commissioners, and so he could efficiently bring under their notice the state of those buildings.

"From what I have observed I am satisfied," he says, "that many existing workhouses are extremely deficient in space, ventilation, and drainage."

The overcrowding in the dormitories is especially pointed out. He writes :—

"In going over the Whitechapel Workhouse I was struck with the statement of the fact that, out of 104 children (girls) resident in that house, 89 have recently been attacked with fever. On examining the dormitory in which these children sleep, my wonder ceased. In a room 88 feet long, 16½ wide, and 7 feet high, with a sloping roof rising to 10 feet, all these 104 children, together with four women who have the charge of them, sleep. The beds are close to each other; in all the beds there are never less than four children, in many five; the ventilation of the room is most imperfect. Under such circumstances the breaking out of fever is inevitable.

"I was likewise struck with the pale and unhealthy appearance of a number of children in the Whitechapel Workhouse, in a room called the 'Infant Nursery.' These children appear to be from two to three years of age; they are 23 in number, they all sleep in one room, and they seldom or never go out of this room either for air or exercise. Several attempts have been made to send these infants into the country, but a majority of the Board of Guardians has hitherto succeeded in resisting the proposition.

"In the Whitechapel Workhouse there are two fever - wards : in the lower ward the beds are much too close ; two fever patients are placed in each bed ; the ventilation is most imperfect, and the room is so close as to be dangerous to all who enter it, as well as most injurious to the sick."

The Report mentions, in contrast, the case of the Jews' Hospital, where he had been physician. In that hospital, though at one time there had been a yearly outbreak of fever, since the number of beds in the dormitories had been reduced, and several large ventilators had been put in, the evil had entirely ceased. At the time he wrote eight years had passed since the improvements, and fever had not once returned as an epidemic.

After finishing this Report, my grandfather set to work to obtain exact statistics as to fever in other parts of London ; and by the next year (1839) tables had been compiled, which proved, by a wider range of experience, the truths he had again and again brought forward. Once more he wrote a Report to the Poor Law Commissioners —of whom Mr (afterwards Sir Edwin) Chadwick was one — pointing out the facts which were proved by these figures and the duty of acting on them.[1]

Such accounts as those given by the three physicians appointed by the Poor Law Board to inquire, could not pass unnoticed. The press, not only in London but in all parts of England, took up the subject. Public men began to be roused.

At first the facts were doubted. It was difficult to believe that such a dreadful state of things *could* exist; but attention was awakened, and inquiry followed.

The Marquis of Normanby, then Secretary of State for the Home Department, was much impressed with what he had read, but he could hardly conquer a belief that there must have been some exaggeration. My grandfather took him to see some of the places in Bethnal Green and Whitechapel which the Report had described. Lord Normanby was deeply moved, as every one must have been who was brought to realise the kind of dwellings which were all that these people had for homes. "So far," he said, "from any

[1] Report on the Prevalence of Fever in Twenty Metropolitan Unions in 1838.

exaggeration having crept into the descriptions which had been given, they had not conveyed to my mind an adequate idea of the truth."

Lord Ashley, too, always in the forefront to relieve the sufferings of the poor, was taken by my grandfather on two occasions to see these regions personally; and from that time forth he became one of the most ardent supporters of the Sanitary Cause, working strenuously for it both in and out of Parliament.[1] In a letter to a friend my grandfather writes :—

"FINSBURY SQUARE, 1841.

"I have just returned from Whitechapel and Bethnal Green, over which I have been taking Lord Ashley and his brother, and I think they have received an impression which will be lasting, and which will stimulate them to exert themselves for the removal of some of the evils which they have witnessed."

The Bishop of London had the honour of being the first to bring the question before Parliament.

[1] For the account of what was shown to Lord Ashley on these occasions see Appendix I., p. 159.

In an earnest and eloquent speech made in the House of Lords during the session of 1839, he moved for an extension of such inquiries as the Poor Law Board had caused to be made in London, to other towns in the United Kingdom.

It must have seemed to my grandfather a glorious moment when the principles he had so long advocated were for the first time recognised —when the country began to hear with surprise and shame of the existing state of things—and when the suffering, which he felt so deeply, seemed about to be relieved.

The movement had now begun. Surely it would go quickly, since the saving of thousands of lives each year depended on its progress ?

CHAPTER VI.

PHILANTHROPIC AND MEDICAL WORK, 1840–1848.

I HAVE now arrived at the period of my grandfather's life which comes within my own memory,
and which begins with the days described in the
Introduction when I used to watch him as he sat
at his writing in the early mornings. He had
taken me to live with him at three years old, and
from that time I was with him throughout his life.
If, in this chapter or elsewhere, I dwell on his care
and tenderness towards myself, it is only that it
may indicate the love he invariably showed to all
near and dear to him.

My grandfather, though losing no opportunity
of promoting the cause he had chiefly at heart—
the great sanitary cause—did not limit his public
work to it alone : he was at this time engaged in
reforming the state of coal-mines, being a member

Old woman carrying coal.

of a Royal Commission—the "Children's Employment Commission" — the chief object of whose
labours was to secure the abolition of child-labour
in mines. It has been mentioned that the Report
presented to Parliament by this Commission had
pictures : they were drawn on the spot at my
grandfather's instigation, and I believe I am right
in saying it was the only parliamentary report so
issued. The state of things in the mines was
sufficiently appalling. Children of tender years
were employed in opening and shutting little
gates in narrow passages of coal. They were
untaught, and seldom breathed the fresh air.
They were sometimes as young as five years
old (parents have been known to send them
even at four years old) ; they sat in small niches,
scooped out of the coal, for twelve hours at a
time, to watch the doors, and they were alone and
in the dark except when a "hurrier" with a
candle fastened to his forehead passed along, on
hands and knees, dragging a truck..

The suffering was not confined to children ; it
was found that young girls, married women, and
aged and decrepit women were exposed to bearing upon their backs burdens of coal weighing

from three-quarters of a cwt. to 3 cwt. ; often to carry these whilst wading in water up to the ankles, sometimes up to the knees, or to carry them from the bottom of the mine to the bank up steep ladders; to go through the hard work of hewing coal by the side of the men; to drag trucks on all fours harnessed by chains ; and that the nature of their work, when hewing coal, constantly obliged them to dispense with most of their clothing.

The illustrations in the Report brought all this before my childish imagination very vividly. Perhaps they also, as the Commissioners hoped they might do, caught the attention of busy members of Parliament and learned lords who might not have waded through a lengthy "blue-book" to find the facts which these pictures showed at a glance. The object of the Commissioners was to put the facts strikingly, and in this they succeeded.

Lord Ashley's Bill, based on this Report, encountered great opposition, especially in the House of Lords, many members of which were large proprietors of mines, and in the course of its passage through Parliament it was much

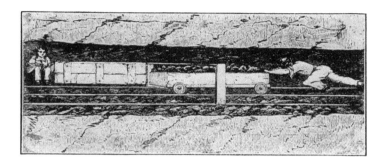

Children at work.

Woman drawing truck.

mutilated. Lord Ashley had hoped to prevent
any boy under thirteen from working in the
mines, but the age of exemption was lowered
to ten years old; and his attempt to prohibit
the employment of boys and old men in the
work of lowering the miners into the pit by
means of ropes was also defeated.

Still, the main points were gained; for by
Lord Ashley's Bill, which passed in 1844 and
was founded on the labours of this and the Factory Commission, not only was it enacted that
all *children* under ten should henceforth be prohibited from working in mines, but that such
labour should also be illegal for girls of all ages
and for women.

It may be worth noticing that the change in
the law did not at first give satisfaction to the
miners. The men considered it a great hardship
to be deprived of the earnings of their wives and
children, and the women themselves complained
sorely of being deprived of their work. But
time has proved the great benefits of the new
system. The men now earn nearly as much as
a man and his wife used to do, the presence
of the wife in the home causes it to be better

cared for, and the children are free to attend school.

The "Children's Employment Commission" instituted a further inquiry into the state of young people employed in branches of trade not as yet brought under regulation. This second Report of the Commission, on "Trades and Manufactures," related to the state of apprentices in the South Staffordshire ironworks, and of young workers in such trades as earthenware-making, calico-printing, paper-making, &c.; and although nothing could be done for them at the time, the regulations recommended in the Report have since been adopted.

These Inquiries—important and interesting as they were—occupied only the hours which my grandfather could spare from his professional work as one of the chief consultants in cases of fever, and a leading London physician.

He went daily from our home in Kentish Town to his rooms in the City, and often used to take me with him as a little child. We usually stopped first at the Fever Hospital, which was then near King's Cross. The Great Northern Railway Station stands now on its site, where I

used to sit in the carriage at its gate. His connection with that Hospital was never broken (at
his death he had been one of its physicians for
nearly forty years), and he was, of course, much
interested in its re-erection when it was removed
to its present position in Liverpool Road, Isling-
ton. The new building was made with wards
having no upper storeys; each ward had three
outer walls and a very high ceiling, thus ensuring
perfect ventilation; and there were many other
advantages of arrangement.

But even the original hospital at King's Cross
was very carefully managed as to fresh air, and
my grandfather's implicit belief in his own doc-
trine of non-contagion was proved by his more
than once taking me into the fever-wards, though,
when I was a child and therefore peculiarly sus-
ceptible, he never would let me breathe the
tainted air of the courts and lanes of which he
fearlessly encountered the danger, not only in his
capacity as a physician, but when making his
early sanitary investigations.

Three times in the course of his life he had
been stricken down with fever. In one of these
attacks his life had been despaired of, but medi-

cal skill, aided by most careful nursing and by
his naturally strong constitution, at length conquered the disease.

After the visit to the hospital we went on into
the City to his consulting-rooms, which were first
at 36 New Broad Street, and afterwards at 38
Finsbury Square; and then came the morning
hours during which he saw patients there, and I
amused myself until he was ready for the afternoon round. Then outdoor work again. Generally the visits led us through crowded streets
where the carriage got blocked in amongst great
waggons or hemmed in near high warehouses;
but at times there came long drives to some
patient living more in the country at Hackney,
Dalston, Stoke Newington, or farther off still;
and then what a happy time I had with him,
sitting on his knee and asking endless questions!
It was worth many hours of waiting in the carriage, outside doors, to have the times that came
between.

Then there was the Eastern Dispensary and
Jews' Hospital practice, in connection with which
he daily went to see patients in their own poor
homes. How well I remember being left in the

carriage at the end of streets too narrow for it to
drive down. I used to amuse myself with looking
out at the people passing to and fro—children
without hats and bonnets ; old-clothesmen with
their bags ; orange-girls ; — many dark faces
amongst the passers-by—Jews, as I was afterwards told. I used to wonder at it all, and make
up stories about the people and guess on what
errands they were bent when entering their little
shops and doorways ; and when tired of all this—
for I was still too small to see without kneeling
up on the seat to look out at the window—I
seated myself on the floor of the carriage and
was soon deeply engrossed in some book of
pictures or fairy tales, which my grandfather, in
the midst of all else, had thoughtfully put into
the pocket of the carriage for me to "find."

Then I would climb up again and watch for
him. At last he would come! Down the dark,
narrow street, looking very grave, the reflection
of some scene just left still resting on his face.
Out of such thoughts—produced by such places
—came his afterwork.

When he came to me, however, the sad
thoughts passed away, and he was ready to let

his happy nature come through to cheer his little girl. He would practically work to relieve such misery as he had seen — day and night — at all cost—through all opposition,—but he would also play merrily with his little grandchild, to make joyous for her the homeward drive through the evening air.

My grandfather was much interested at this time in another effort of which I have not yet spoken. It was the institution of a "Home in Sickness" in London for those of the middle classes who might be far from their own families, or who, from some other cause, could not secure favourable surroundings in times of illness. The position of such people struck him as very desolate. There were many with homes far away— clerks, students, young men engaged in various professions, governesses, and other ladies of limited income—who might be seized with illness under circumstances when a return to their family was impossible; others who had no family to which to return. It seemed to him that chambers or lodgings which might be tolerably convenient for people in health, were utterly unsuited to give the requisite comforts when illness came : the poorer classes had the hospitals, but for this intermediate class there was no provision.

His plan was, therefore, to found an institution into which, by subscribing a small sum annually, members could secure a right to be received when they were suffering from disease. They would each have a separate room where an equal temperature could be secured, well prepared diet, superior nursing, the advantage of a medical officer in the house who could be called in at any moment, and the daily advice of skilled physicians and surgeons specially appointed ; or should the patients prefer it, of their own medical advisers. For this they were to pay two guineas a-week during their residence, or less, should it be found that such an establishment could be self-supporting at a lower rate : that it should be self-supporting was, he thought, essential.

Such an institution was founded in 1840 under very good auspices, and opened under the name of " The Sanatorium " at Devonshire House, York Gate, Regent's Park, in 1842. My grandfather freely gave it his medical services, as well as his influence and supervision, for some years.

The house stood in a garden in which there were tall trees (with rooks in them), making a cool green shade and shutting out all other houses; whilst within doors the soft carpets and general feeling of quiet and order gave a sense of peace. The contrast on turning into that garden from the "New Road"[1] was striking. Quiet, indeed, was one of the chief boons which the Sanatorium could offer.

Charles Dickens, one of its earliest supporters, speaks forcibly of this contrast in a speech made in behalf of the Institution. He speaks of the noise of crowded streets and busy thoroughfares as—

"That never-ceasing restlessness, that incessant tread of feet wearing the rough stones smooth and glossy." "Is it not a wonder," he says,—"is it not a wonder, how the dwellers in narrow ways can bear it? Think of a sick man in such a place as St Martin's Court, listening to the footsteps, and in the midst of pain and weariness obliged, despite himself (as though it were a task he must perform), to detect the child's step from the man's; the slipshod beggar from the hooded exquisite;

[1] Now Marylebone Road.

the lounging from the busy. Think of the hum and noise always present to his senses, and of the stream of life that will not stop, pouring on, on, on, through all his restless dreams, as if he were condemned to lie dead, but conscious, in a noisy churchyard, and had no hope of rest for centuries to come."

After some time it was found that a building specially constructed, which should contain many small separate rooms, would be more suitable and less expensive than Devonshire House. To erect this it was necessary to raise a building fund. By this time the Institution was supported by a powerful list of patrons, with Prince Albert at their head; many large banking-houses and City firms had subscribed to it for the sake of their clerks and others; and more than a hundred members of the medical profession had visited it, and had signed a statement expressing their belief in the need of such an establishment, adding that the Sanatorium had supplied this need most satisfactorily, though on a small scale.

Charles Dickens then lived nearly opposite to Devonshire House, and when the building fund was opened, he and several other literary men and artists came forward and gave for its benefit the first of those amateur performances which they repeated at a later period. They acted Ben Jonson's "Every Man in his Humour," at St James's Theatre, on November 15, 1845, both audience and actors being brilliant. Charles Dickens, Douglas Jerrold, John Foster, Mark Lemon, Frank Stone, and others took part. I remember seeing them, as I peeped down from a side-box.

The Sanatorium did not, from a money point of view, succeed; but it was, nevertheless, the forerunner of all those "Home Hospitals" and "Nursing Homes" which have since proved so great a boon to the public. So that in this, also, my grandfather was a pioneer.

As the name of Dickens has been mentioned, it may be interesting to refer here to some of the letters which show the early and keen interest he felt in the removal of the evils with which my grandfather was contending, and his readiness to give his aid to the cause of the poor. Here is the first letter, alluding both to the Sanatorium and to the Children's Employment Commission :—

1 Devonshire Terrace York Gate
fifteenth December 1840.

My dear Sir

I am greatly obliged to
you for your kind note and
inclosure of today. I had
never seen the Sanatorium pamphlet, and have been greatly
pleased with it The reasons
for such an Institution and
the advantages likely to result
from it, could not have been more
forcibly or eloquently put. I have
read it twice with extreme satisfaction.

You have given me hardly
less pleasure by sending me

the Instructions of the childrens' imployment commission, which seem to me to have been devised in a most worthy spirit, and to comprehend every point on which humanity and forethought could have desired to lay stress. The little book reached me very opportunely; for Lord Ashley sent me his speech on moving the commission only the day before yesterday and I could not forbear, in writing to him in acknowledgment of its receipt, cursing the present system and its fatal effects in keeping down thousands upon thousands of God's images, with all my heart and soul.

It must be a great comfort and happiness to you to be instrumental in bringing about so much good. I am proud to be remembered by one who is pursuing such ends.

and heartily hope that we shall
know each other better.

My dear Sir

Faithfully yours

Charles Dickens

D. Southwood Smith.

1 DEVONSHIRE TERRACE, YORK GATE,
Fifteenth December 1840.

MY DEAR SIR,—I am greatly obliged to you for your kind note and inclosure of to-day. I had never seen the Sanatorium pamphlet, and have been greatly pleased with it. The reasons for such an Institution, and the advantages likely to result from it, could not have been more forcibly or eloquently put. I have read it twice with extreme satisfaction.

You have given me hardly less pleasure by sending me the Instructions of the Children's Employment Commission, which seem to me to have been devised in a most worthy spirit, and to comprehend every point on which humanity and forethought could have desired to lay stress. The little book reaches me very opportunely; for Lord Ashley sent me his speech on moving the Commission only the day before yesterday; and I could not forbear, in writing to him in acknowledgment of its receipt, cursing the present system and its fatal effects in keeping down thousands upon thousands of God's images, with all my heart and soul.

It must be a great comfort and happiness to

you to be instrumental in bringing about so much good. I am proud to be remembered by one who is pursuing such ends, and heartily hope that we shall know each other better.—My dear Sir, faithfully yours, CHARLES DICKENS.

Dr SOUTHWOOD SMITH.

Another characteristic and genial letter, dated half a-year later, appears to refer to some proposed expedition, in the course of which Dickens was to see on the spot some place where children were at work in a coal-mine :—

DEVONSHIRE TERRACE,
Wednesday, June the Second, 1841.

MY DEAR DR SMITH,—I find it can't be done. The artists, engravers, printers, and every one engaged have so depended on my promises, and so fashioned their engagements by them, that I cannot with any regard to their comfort or convenience leave town before the nineteenth. At any other time I would have gone with you to John-o'-Groat's for such a purpose; and I don't thank you the less heartily for not being able to go now.

If you should see one place which you would

like me to behold of all others, and should find
that I could get easy access to it, tell me when
you come back, and I'll see it on my way to
Scotland, please God.

I will send your papers home by hand to-
morrow.—In haste, believe me with true regards,
faithfully yours, CHARLES DICKENS.

Dr SOUTHWOOD SMITH.

The following year, Dickens, being about to
proceed to Cornwall, wrote to my grandfather
asking his advice as follows :—

DEVONSHIRE TERRACE,
Saturday, October Twenty-second, 1842.

MY DEAR SIR,—I have an expedition afoot
in which I think you can assist me.

I want to see the very dreariest and most
desolate portion of the sea - coast of Cornwall ;
and start next Thursday, with a couple of friends,
for St Michael's Mount. Can you tell me of
your own knowledge, or through the information
of any of the Mining Sub-Commissioners, what
is the next best bleak and barren part ? And
can you, furthermore, while I am in those regions,
help me down a mine ?

I ought to make many apologies for troubling you, but somehow or other I don't—which is your fault and not mine.—Always believe me faithfully your friend,   CHARLES DICKENS.

Dr SOUTHWOOD SMITH.

My grandfather's feeling about the Cornish coast is given in his answer :—

                         36 NEW BROAD STREET, *October* 25, 1842.

MY DEAR SIR,—I do not think you will find St Michael's Mount particularly desolate, but it is nevertheless a very remarkable and interesting place. The coast about Land's End, I am told, is incomparably more dreary and presents a fine specimen of wrecken scenery. But the place above all others for dreariness is Tintagel (King Arthur's) Castle, near Camelford. There shall you see nothing but bleak-looking rocks and an everlastingly boisterous sea, both in much the same state as when good King Arthur reigned.[1]

You must go through Truro to get to either

---

[1] It is somewhat curious to note that a similar enthusiasm for Tintagel animated the mind of his granddaughter, Octavia Hill : she became instrumental, through the National Trust, in preserving its wonderful cliff intact for the nation for ever. It was bought in 1896.

place. Your best plan will be to call on Dr Charles Barham. He is the physician of those parts and a most intelligent man, thoroughly acquainted with every nook in Cornwall and known to every mine. He was one of our best Sub-Commissioners; and he will tell you where best to go for your immediate object, and will take you with the least loss of time to the best specimen of a mine. But pray do not forget that a Cornish mine is quite different from a coal-mine: while much less disagreeable to the senses, far more fatal in its effects upon the men and boys (they have no women).

I send you herewith a letter of introduction to Dr Barham, whom you will find both able and willing to give you all the information and assistance you may require.—Faithfully yours,

SOUTHWOOD SMITH.

The following merry letter from Dickens, on his return, winds up the little correspondence :—

1 DEVONSHIRE TERRACE,
YORK GATE, *Eighth November* 1842.

MY DEAR SIR,—I have just come home from Cornwall. I did not, after all, deliver your letter.

Having Stanfield and Maclise and another friend with me, I determined not to do so, unless I found it absolutely necessary; lest the unfortunate Doctor should consider himself in a state of siege.

I saw all I wanted to see, and a noble coast it is. I have sent your letter to Dr Barham with a line or two from myself; and am as much obliged to you as though I had driven him wild with trouble.—Always faithfully yours,

CHARLES DICKENS.

Dr SOUTHWOOD SMITH.

Before leaving this subject, I will give two more of Charles Dickens's letters, which show that the interest he had manifested in the first beginning of the inquiry into the state of the children in coal-pits did not wane, but that, when the Report came before him in 1843, he was deeply moved, and prepared himself at once to take up arms in defence of the children. The first letter runs thus :—

DEVONSHIRE TERRACE, *Sixth March* 1843.

MY DEAR DR SMITH,—I sent a message across the way to-day, urging you, in case you should come to the Sanatorium, to call on me if convenient. My reason was this :

I am so perfectly stricken down by the bluebook you have sent me, that I think (as soon as I shall have done my month's work) of writing and bringing out a very cheap pamphlet called "An Appeal to the People of England on behalf of the Poor Man's Child," with my name attached, of course.

I should be very glad to take counsel with you in the matter, and to receive any suggestions from you in reference to it. Suppose I were to call on you one evening in the course of ten days or so ? What would be the most likely hour to find you at home ? — In haste, always faithfully your friend,   CHARLES DICKENS.

Dr SOUTHWOOD SMITH.

The next promises a "sledge-hammer" in lieu of the pamphlet.

DEVONSHIRE TERRACE, *Tenth March* 1843.

MY DEAR DR SMITH, — Don't be frightened when I tell you that, since I wrote to you last, reasons have presented themselves for deferring the production of that pamphlet until the end

of the year. I am not at liberty to explain them
further just now ; but *rest assured* that when you
know them, and see what I do, and where and how,
you will certainly feel that a sledge-hammer has
come down with twenty times the force—twenty
thousand times the force I could exert by following out my first idea. Even so recently as
when I wrote to you the other day I had not
contemplated the means I shall now, please God,
use. But they have been suggested to me ; and
I have girded myself for their seizure—as you
shall see in due time.

If you will allow our *tête-à-tête* and projected
conversation on the subject still to come off, I will
write to you as soon as I see my way to the
end of my month's work. — Always faithfully
yours,   CHARLES DICKENS.

Dr SOUTHWOOD SMITH.

I now turn to another subject. It was during these years that my grandfather conceived
the idea that houses might be built from which
fever could be banished even amongst the classes
and in the districts in which up to that time
disease had most fatally prevailed. If the ex-

periment succeeded, and the amount of sickness
and death were found to be markedly diminished,
he felt that a very valuable practical illustration
would be afforded of the truth of the principles he
was advocating—of the law which connects bad
sanitary conditions with disease. He also hoped
it would be proved that money expended on the
building of such dwellings would bring in a fair
return of interest, so that it would be seen to
be a wise as well as a benevolent expenditure of
capital, and healthy dwellings might be multiplied.

To accomplish this purpose he gathered together the men who formed the original direc-
tors of "The Metropolitan Association for Improving the Dwellings of the Industrious
Classes" in 1843.

As this was before the days of "limited lia-
bility," it was necessary to obtain through the
Prime Minister a Royal Charter to secure those
who should furnish money for the experiment
against serious loss if it failed, and a depu-
tation (who chose my grandfather as spokes-
man) waited on Sir Robert Peel on January
23, 1844, to ask him for this charter, which
was eventually cordially granted.

The course the promoters took resulted in the building of the block of, so-called, "Model Dwellings" in Old St Pancras Road, on a site nearly opposite the Fever Hospital.

Thus a first step was taken towards providing healthy and cheap homes for the poor, and the results realised the fullest hopes of the originators.

In 1844 we removed from Kentish Town to our Highgate home. It was very beautifully situated, the slopes of the West Hill lying at the back, and the front looking over Caen Wood. When we went there, not even the present open park paling divided us from the park : there were only a few moss-grown and picturesque hurdles bordering the road between us and it, and our lane was as quiet as if it had been far in the real country. The life was, indeed, like that of the country, and full of pleasure to a child. We had cows; and my longed-for and much-enjoyed pony in the field; and chickens, and dogs, and a goat, and pigs; a perfect orchard of wonderful apple-trees, and a wealth of roses that I have never seen equalled. In the summer came hay-making of our own, and all this so near London that half an hour's drive of our fast horse Ariel took us to its centre. It was indeed inwardly and outwardly a beautiful home, and it is *the* one of my childhood which is fullest of recollections of my grandfather. During all my early years he had, as it were, *two* works going on—the profession which occupied his days, and the work for the various reforms, which occupied the early mornings and the quiet Sundays alluded to in the Introduction. But now, as the "ten years' struggle" advanced, the necessity of attending committees and of having interviews with public men, whom he was interesting and bringing together, made itself felt; and thus not only were the early mornings, as hitherto, given up, but, as the public health cause advanced, many hours were given out of his professional time, and he compressed that given to his practice as much as possible. He worked enthusiastically, and with unfailing energy, beginning to write at four or five (sometimes even at three) o'clock in the morning, and only returning home to dinner about eight o'clock in the evening.

Our "Hillside" was a peaceful and lovely spot for him to come to after the day's work in London, and he made the most of the hours spent at home. It was his wish, and our habit, during all possible weather to breakfast out in the summer-house, which stood at the top of that piece of Lord Mansfield's park which was our field, so that he might carry the memory of its pretty view, and the feeling of its fresh morning air, into town with him. We dined in the garden in a tent under trees and surrounded by flower-beds, and had dessert in the field, where the view of the wooded slopes in the light of the setting sun gave much delight, not only to ourselves, but to many of the distinguished friends who frequently joined us on those happy evenings. These hours were indeed happy ones, whether in summer, spent in the field out in the starlight, or in winter, round his hospitable fire; for he liked to have, and helped to make, happiness around him.

Sometimes he used to let me tell him the story of my day—the wonderful doings of pony, dog, or newly-hatched little yellow chickens.

And then he would tell us of his own work. Each time that some onward step of importance had been taken he told us about it, but when things were uncertain, or depressing, he seldom mentioned them. So that an advance for the cause came generally with the pleasure of a sudden surprise, but a defeat we only surmised by seeing him unusually grave. He was naturally extremely reserved; but as he advanced in years his desire for sympathy overcame this reticence in some degree, so that he became ready to share his thoughts on all deep subjects with others. He rarely spoke of things merely personal, and there was an absence of all littleness in his conversation which was striking. A mixture of high thought with simplicity of expression was characteristic of him. I listened to all that passed, and with a strange, vague, but gradually - increasing understanding, I learned to watch for the success of his different efforts.

The days were over when the height of the carriage-windows had been an obstacle to my view out into the streets of Whitechapel in our daily drives, but I was still a child at the

G

time of the first public meeting of the "Health of Towns Association." To this day the look of everything at that meeting is distinctly impressed upon me : the platform ; the empty chairs upon it ; the table and bottle of water ; the crowd round us, which were all new to me, are remembered as vivid first impressions are. And when, after waiting some time, a number of men came in — many of them of great importance — and I saw my grandfather amongst them, how proud and glad I felt that his efforts to interest others had been successful, and that he now had all this strength on his side.

I did not understand all that passed, but I knew when the speakers praised him ; and when his speech came, towards the end of the meeting, I felt the thrill of his voice, and liked all those other people to hear it too—I liked them to feel *what* he was.

But stronger even than the pride in him was the belief that people must be moved by the truth that was being brought forward ; for, even more than himself, I loved his cause. He lost himself in it, and I caught from him the desire, above all else, for the progress of the thing itself.

It is pleasant to me now to see the words, only partly understood then, in which the public men with whom he worked expressed the feeling with which he inspired them. "Benevolent," "earnest," "indefatigable,"—this is what they call him when mentioning his name. Again and again he was thanked in the House of Commons and House of Lords for what he had done.

"The country was indebted to Dr Southwood Smith and Mr Slaney," says Sir Robert Harry Inglis, M.P., "for its first knowledge of the real condition of the poorer classes. Their unwearied labours for the instruction of the Legislature and the public on these subjects were unrewarded by emolument or fame; though the value of their services was beginning to be appreciated, and they would be more highly estimated by posterity than in their own day."

And Mr Slaney himself says that "for the powerful manner in which he had first described the actual condition of the poor in their present dwellings; for the clearness with which he had shown that their most grievous sufferings were adventitious and removable; and for the untiring zeal with which he had continued to press these

truths on the attention of the Legislature and
the public, Dr Southwood Smith deserved the
gratitude of his country."

In bringing in the first sanitary measure in
1841, Lord Normanby speaks of what Dr Southwood Smith had "taught" him; and in 1847 the
same tone is still used.

In bringing in the Health of Towns Bill in
1848, Lord Morpeth, then Home Secretary,
gracefully disclaims his own share in the work,
and alludes to my grandfather, amongst others,
when saying,—

"Several persons of very great accomplishment, and, what is more to the purpose, of most
ardent benevolence, both in and out of this House,
have taken great pains, in a way which does
them infinite credit, to inform and excite the
public mind on this subject ; and now, mainly by
the accident of my position, I find myself at the
last hour (as I trust it may prove to be) entering
upon the fruit of their labours and gleaning from
their stores."

All they could say of his devotion to the cause
of the people and the saving of life was true.
Silently, almost unconsciously, and as the most

natural thing he could do, he pursued his point. As far as unceasing labour could enable him, he carried on both his professional and his public work; but when it became a question between private fortune and public good he never hesitated — he steadily and persistently chose the latter.

CHAPTER VII.

THE TEN YEARS' STRUGGLE FOR SANITARY REFORM, 1838–1848.

IT is not easy to convince a whole nation of the truth of new principles, however closely they may in reality affect its welfare; not easy to produce a degree of conviction that shall lead to practical, tangible results. The early workers in the public movements, such as that for Sanitary Reform, have first to spread such a knowledge of existing evils as shall create a general feeling of the need for improvement. They have to educate the public until it believes in that need. And when the *vis inertia* of ignorance and indifference is overcome, they have to encounter the active opposition of those whose interests are bound up with the old abuses, and whose property would be affected were the evil swept away. Even when it is decided that something must be done they have to bear a long time of waiting until it is settled what that something is to be, for decision is not easy when questions arise which closely affect the property of a powerful class.

From these causes arose the long delay which occurred before any mitigation of the suffering took place, and hence it was that the great feature of the period was a succession of " Inquiries " and of bills brought before Parliament and defeated.

The first step in the House of Commons was made in 1840, the year following that which has just been spoken of as the one from which dates the public beginning of the Sanitary movement, when Mr Slaney, M.P. (one of the most earnest and energetic of the early labourers in the cause) obtained a Committee of the House to " inquire into the sanitary state of large towns in England." Mr Slaney wished not only to extend the investigation, but to bring the striking results already obtained directly before Parliament.

My grandfather was the first witness examined by the Committee, and nearly the whole of his evidence was transferred to its minutes. Some of his words were—

" *These miseries will continue till the Gov-ernment will pass measures which shall remove the sources of poison and disease from these places. All this suffering might be averted. These poor people are victims that are sacri-ficed. The effect is the same as if twenty or thirty thousand of them were annually taken out of their wretched homes and put to death; the only difference being that they are left in them to die.*"

And how long was it before any measure to stop this could be carried through Parlia-ment? Dating from the time when he first examined Bethnal Green and Whitechapel, *ten years.* Not long, perhaps, in reality, consider-ing the difficulties in the way, but very long to one who not only believed, but most deeply felt and realised, the truth of such words as those quoted above.

The history of events was this. In 1841 Lord Normanby brought in a " Drainage of Buildings Bill." It was by no means a perfect one. My grandfather wrote of it many years afterwards in the following words :—

" Subsequent discussion and inquiry greatly

3 Trafalgar Square
Jan.ʸ 25ᵗʰ 1841.

My Lord

I have collected & arranged
for you some Evidence shewing
the necessity of Sanatory Regulations,
in Towns, which I think will
interest you, & I hope in some
degree assist you in your beneficent
undertaking. I trust the measure
you are about to introduce for
the protection of the Health of the
Poor,(1) will constitute & will be

1. Drainage of Buildings Bill. First direct attempt at
Sanitary Legislation. – Introduced by the Marquis of
Normanby in 1841. S. L.

recognized hereafter, as the second
great legislative Enactment for
their benefit, as the Act of Queen
Elizabeth was the first; & that the
second will be found in practice
to produce far more extensive &
unmixed good.

I should be glad of an opportunity
of explaining one or two points to
your Lordship without inconvenience if you could see
me at any time for a few minutes.
I am My Lord
    With great respect
    Your obliged & faithful Servt—
        Southwood Smith.

improved both the principles and the details of sanitary legislation as compared with the proposals in this bill. Still, honour to the House of Lords who carried it with a cordial and noble spirit through their own House and sent it down to the Commons!"

The session, however, came to an end before any discussion could there be held on it.

Next year, 1842, was presented Mr Edwin Chadwick's Report on the Sanitary Condition of the Labouring Population of Great Britain. He was Secretary to the Poor Law Board, and this Report was, in fact, a Return to the Bishop of London's motion of 1839. It confirmed and extended the results of previous inquiries, and greatly helped to prepare the way for legislation.

In 1843 Lord Normanby made a second attempt. It was again defeated. The Administration of which he was a member was broken up before much progress had been made with the new and improved bill which he had introduced.

Now came another Inquiry. Sir Robert Peel's Government, soon after coming into office, appointed a Royal Commission,[1] of which the Duke

---

[1] "The Health of Towns Commission."

of Buccleuch was chairman, "to inquire into the state of large towns and populous districts." My grandfather was again the first witness examined. Their report was presented in June 1844; but during this session no bill bearing on sanitary subjects was even introduced.

My grandfather, however, who was brought daily face to face with the preventible suffering, was not likely to forget it, nor to relax his efforts. With the calm, persistent earnestness which was characteristic of him, he worked on and on. The more defeats, the more necessity for strenuous exertion.

Seeing the difficulty of obtaining any practical result from all the labour that had been devoted to the improvement of the health of the people, he now determined to try to bring together the distinguished men who had taken an interest in the cause, and who had exerted themselves to promote it. He hoped that, thus united, they would have more power in spreading the information which had been acquired, and in forcing it on the attention of the public and the Legislature; and he also thought that a body of men acquainted with the subject would be useful

Mr Slaney, M.P.   Mr Bouverie.   Mr C. Cochrane.   Lord Ebrington, M.P.
             Dr Guy.   Lord Ashley, M.P.   The Marquis of Normanby.   Mr Baines, M.P.   Mr Cardwell, M.P.   Mr Shafto Ad
outhwood Smith.

FIRST MEETING OF THE HEALTH OF TOWNS ASSOCIATION.

(FROM AN OLD PRINT.)

in suggesting and discussing remedies, and in proposing legislative measures.

He succeeded in this effort. He founded the " Health of Towns Association " already referred to, which, numbering amongst its members Lord Normanby, Lord Ashley, Lord Morpeth, Lord Robert Grosvenor, Lord Ebrington, Mr Slaney, M.P., and many other influential men both in and out of Parliament, proved a highly useful instrument in carrying forward the work of Sanitary Reform up to the time of the passing of the Public Health Act.

Its first meeting was held in December 1844, and the facts which the various speakers eloquently brought out are chiefly summed up in the petition which, in accordance with one of the resolutions then passed, was presented to Parliament.

Those to whom sanitary truths are familiar will have little interest in this repetition of what they already know, except as showing what the early sanitary work was before a public opinion had been formed. But it is somewhat curious to look back upon a time when it was necessary to state what now appear self-evident truths.

My grandfather gives it as the opinion of the
meeting, that—

"From the neglect of sewerage, drainage, a
due supply of water, air, and light to the interior
of houses, and an efficient system of house and
street cleansing, a poisonous atmosphere is en-
gendered, particularly in the districts occupied
by the poor, which endangers the health and life
of the whole community, but which is particularly injurious to the industrious classes.

"That it appears from indubitable evidence
that the amount of deaths attributable to these
causes is, in England alone, upwards of 40,000
annually.[1]

"That the great majority of the persons who
thus prematurely perish are between the ages of

---

[1] The statements as to the saving of life which would be effected
if proper sanitary measures were carried out were necessarily
various, since the difference which could be made in the death-rate
was a matter of opinion, and had yet to be proved by experiment.
If, instead of one death annually in every 46 inhabitants throughout England and Wales (the then proportion), there should be an
improvement sufficient to secure there being one death in every
50, upwards of 25,000 lives would be saved. Whilst, if the sanitary
state of towns could be raised to that of healthy counties, there
would be a saving of 49,000 lives. The Association seems to have
chosen something between the least probable and the highest
probable saving of life.—G. L.

twenty and forty, the period when they ought to be most capable of labour and are heads of families ; and that it appears from official returns that in some districts nearly one-third of the poor-rates are expended in the maintenance of destitute widows and orphans rendered destitute by the premature death of adult males : that the number of widows receiving out-relief was, in the year 1844, 86,000; that these widows had dependent upon them 111,000 orphan children ; and that there were, besides, receiving relief in the Union houses, 18,000 orphan children.

"That the expense thus constantly incurred for the maintenance of the destitute would in many cases defray the cost of putting the district into a good sanitary condition, and thus prevent the recurrence of these dreadful evils.

That this poisonous atmosphere, even when not sufficient to destroy life, undermines the strength, deteriorates the constitution, and renders the labourer in a great degree unable to work ; and that there is every reason to believe that his healthy life and working ability is abridged in many districts to the extent of twelve years. And lastly—

" That the moral and religious improvement of the industrious classes is incompatible with such a degree of physical degradation as is actually prevalent in numerous instances ; and that until the dwellings of the poor are rendered capable of affording the comforts of a home, the earnest and best directed efforts of the schoolmaster and clergyman must in a great degree be in vain."

In 1845 the Government Commission issued their second Report. Another bill, founded on this and their former Report, was brought forward ; but it was so late in the year that it could not be passed that session.

Lord Lincoln, who brought it in, avowed that his principal motive was that it might be considered during the recess. "The Health of Towns Association" was here very useful in publishing a report (addressed in the first instance to its own members) criticising the provisions of this bill. My grandfather wrote this report, assisted by the notes and suggestions of various members, and by Mr Chadwick, who, though not connected with the Association, helped greatly on this and other occasions.

Lord Lincoln's bill was not again introduced,

and the only sign of progress in these matters during 1846 was to be found in the criticisms offered on that abortive measure.

It was at this juncture that it was thought well to strengthen the hands of the Government by bringing the force of Petition to bear upon the Legislature. It thus became important to arouse the attention of the working classes to the subject.

My grandfather, as one move in this direction, wrote the following address, which I give in full. It was written from his heart, and, with all its calm, philosophical mode of expression, burns underneath with the white heat of that earnestness which made this sanitary cause—this saving of life and of suffering—with him almost a crusade.

An Address to the Working Classes of the United Kingdom on their Duty in the Present State of the Sanitary Question.

My Fellow-Countrymen,

The artificial distinctions by which the people of a country are divided into different classes have no relation to the capacities and endowments of our common nature. No class is higher or better than another in the sense of having more or different sentient, intellectual, moral, and religious faculties. Every property by which the human being is distinguished from the other creatures of the earth is possessed alike by rich and poor. Wealth can give to the rich man no additional powers of this kind, nor can poverty deprive the poor man of one of them. Before these glorious gifts with which our common nature is endowed, with which all human beings without distinction are enriched, and which can be neither added to nor taken away, the little distinctions of man's creation sink into absolute insignificance.

It is the universal possession of these noble faculties by the human race that makes the gift of human life alike a boon to all. It is the exercise of these noble faculties on objects appropriate to them, and worthy of them, that *makes* life a boon. It is because these faculties, when duly exercised and properly directed, strengthen and enlarge with time, that the value of life increases with its duration. In the mere possession of the full number of the years that make up the natural term of life there is a larger and higher boon than is apparent at first view. What the natural term of human life may be is indeed altogether unknown; because, although one of the characteristics by which man is distinguished from other animals is, that he is capable of understanding the conditions of his existence, and of exerting, within a certain limit, a control over them, so as to be able materially to shorten or to prolong the actual duration of his life,—yet these conditions have hitherto been so little regarded that there is not a single example on record of a community in which the conditions favourable to life have been present and constant, and in which the conditions unfavourable to it have been excluded, in as complete a degree as is obviously practicable. History is full of instances in which the successive generations of a people have been swept away with extraordinary rapidity; but on no page is there to be found the notice of a single nation, in ancient or modern times, the great mass of the population of which has attained a higher longevity; yet it is certain that a degree of longevity never yet witnessed has always been attainable, because such longevity depends on condi-

H

tions which are now known—conditions entirely within human control.

I have said that there is involved in the mere length of life a larger and higher boon than is apparent without reflection. First, because length of life is in general a tolerably accurate measure of the amount of health, without a good share of which life is comparatively worthless. The instances are rare in which a person attains to old age who has not enjoyed at least a moderate share of daily health and vigour.

Secondly, because length of life is a perfectly accurate measure of the amount of enjoyment. Long life is incompatible with a condition of constant privation and wretchedness. It is one of the beneficences of the constitution of our nature that when the balance of happiness is against us, a limit is fixed to our misery by its rapid termination in the insensibility of death. In the very brevity of its existence, therefore, a human being indicates his own history for evil ; the shortness of his life is the sure and correct index of the amount of his suffering, physical and mental : it is the result, the sum-total, the aggregate expression, of the ills endured.

Thirdly, because length of life is the protraction of that portion of life, and only of that portion of it, in which the human being is capable of the greatest degree of usefulness. I have elsewhere shown that every year by which the term of human life is extended is really added to the period of mature age; the period when the organs of the body have attained their full growth and put forth their full strength; when the physical organisation has acquired its utmost perfection; when the senses, the feelings, the emotions, the passions, the affections are in the highest degree acute, intense, and varied; when the intellectual faculties, completely unfolded and developed, carry on their operations with the greatest vigour, soundness, and continuity : in a word, when the individual is capable of communicating, as well as of receiving, the largest amount of the highest kind of happiness.

These considerations give peculiar interest to the results of the inquiries recently made into the actual duration of life at the present time in our cities, towns, and villages. From these inquiries it appears not only that the rate of mortality in the whole of England at the present day is deplorably high, but that there is an extraordinary excess of mortality over and above what is natural, supposing the term at present attainable to be the natural term of human life. The statement of this excess presents to the mind an appalling picture. From accurate calculations, based on the observation of carefully recorded facts, it is rendered certain that the annual slaughter in England alone by causes that are preventible, by causes that produce only one disease — namely, typhus fever — is more than double the loss sustained by the allied armies in the battle of Waterloo; that 136 persons perish every day in England alone whose lives might be saved; that in one single city—namely, Manchester — thirteen thousand three hundred and sixty-two children have perished in seven years over and above the mortality natural to mankind.

It appears, moreover, that the field in which this annual slaughter takes place is always and everywhere the locality in which you reside, and that it is you and your wives and children who are the victims. In some instances in the streets, courts, and alleys in which you live, the mortality which afflicts you is nearly double, and in others it is quite double, that of the inhabitants of other streets in the same district, and in adjoining districts. While the average age at death of the gentry and of professional persons and their families is forty-four, the average age at death attained by you and your families in many instances is only twenty-two, just one-half,—that is to say, comparing your condition with that of the professional persons, you and your families are deprived of one-half of your natural term of life.

Though the causes by which you and your children are thus immolated are well known ; though they have been constantly proclaimed to the public and the Government for nearly ten years past ; though their truth is universally admitted ; and though it is further admitted that the causes in question are removable,—yet not only has nothing whatever been done to remove them, but their operation during this very year has been far more fatal than at any period since we have had the means of making accurate observations on the subject. Thus we are informed by the Registrar-General, that in the summer quarter of the present year Ten Thousand Lives have been destroyed, in a part only of England, by causes which there is every reason to believe may be removed ; that in the succeeding quarter—namely, the quarter ending the 30th of September —the number of deaths exceeded the number in the corresponding quarter of last year by Fifteen Thousand Two Hundred and Twenty - seven ; that is to say, in the very last quarter upwards of 15,000 persons perished, in a part only of England, beyond the mortality of the corresponding quarter of last year.

From this same report it appears, further, that in many of our large towns and populous districts —that is, in the places in which you in great numbers carry on your daily toil—the mortality has nearly doubled ; in some it has quite doubled, and in others it has actually more than doubled ; that this is the case among other places in Sheffield and Birmingham ; that in Sheffield, for example, the number of deaths in the last quarter are double those in the corresponding quarter of last year and 149 over ; while in Birmingham they are double and 239 over.

" The causes of this high mortality," says the Registrar-General, " have been traced to crowded lodgings, dirty dwellings, personal uncleanliness, and the concentration of unhealthy emanations from narrow streets without fresh air, water, or sewerage."

We are further told by the Registrar-General that "the returns of the past quarter prove that nothing effectual has been done to put a stop to the disease, suffering, and death in which so many thousands perish; that the improvements, chiefly of a showy, superficial, outside character, have not reached the homes and habits of the people; and that the consequence is that thousands, not only of the children, but of the men and women themselves, perish of the diseases formerly so fatal, for the same reason, in barracks, camps, gaols, and ships."

For every one of the lives of these 15,000 persons who have thus perished during the last quarter, and who might have been saved by human agency, those are responsible whose proper office it is to interfere and endeavour to stay the calamity—who have the power to save, but who will not use it. But their apathy is an additional reason why you should rouse yourselves, and show that you will submit to this dreadful state of things no longer. Let a voice come from your

streets, lanes, alleys, courts, workshops, and houses
that shall startle the ear of the public and com-
mand the attention of the Legislature.   The time
is auspicious for the effort ; it is a case in which
it is right that you should take a part, in which
you are bound to take a part, in which your own
interests and the wellbeing of those most dear to
you require you to take a part.   The Government is disposed to espouse your cause ; but
narrow, selfish, short-sighted interests will be
banded against you.   Petition both Houses of
Parliament.   Call upon the instructed and benevolent men in the legislative body to sustain your
just claim to protection and assistance.   Petition
Parliament to give you sewers ; petition Parliament to secure to you constant and abundant
supplies of water—supplies adequate to the un-
intermitting and effectual cleansing both of your
sewers and streets ; petition Parliament to remove
—for it is in the power of Parliament universally
and completely to remove—the sources of poison
that surround your dwellings, and that carry disease, suffering, and death into your homes.   Tell
them of the parish of St Margaret, in Leicester,
with a population of 22,000 persons, almost all of

whom are artisans, and where the average age of death in the whole parish was during the year 1846 only eighteen years ; tell them that on taking the ages of death in the different *streets* in this parish, it was found that in those streets that were drained (and there was not a single street in the place properly drained) the average age of death was twenty-three and a-half years ; that in the streets that were partially drained it was seventeen and a-half years ; while in the streets that were entirely undrained it was only thirteen and a-half years.

You cannot disclose to them the suffering you have endured on your beds of sickness, and by which your wives and children have been hurried to their early graves—there is no column in the tables of the Registrar-General which can show that ; but you can tell them that you know, and you can remind them that they admit, that by proper sanitary regulations the same duration of life may be extended to you and your families that is at present enjoyed by professional persons, and that it is possible to obtain for the whole of a town population at least such an average duration of life as is already experienced in some parts of it. In your workshops, in your clubs, in your institutes, obtain signatures to your petitions : get every labourer, every artisan, every tradesman whom you can influence, to sign petitions. Other things must also be done before your condition can be rendered prosperous ; but this *must* precede every real improvement : the sources of the poison that infects the atmosphere you breathe must be dried up before you can be healthy, and uncleanliness must be removed from the exterior of your dwellings before you can find or make a Home.—I am your friend and servant,

SOUTHWOOD SMITH.

1st January 1847.

In this same year 1847 a Royal Commission— "Metropolitan Sanitary Commission" (of which my grandfather was a member)—was appointed to inquire "whether any, and what, sanitary measures were required for London."

To the country at large, however, it seemed as if perhaps there had been enough "inquiring." The thing *had* been considered. Surely something might be *done ;* and Lord Morpeth now brought forward a Government measure for "improving the health of towns in England."

In bringing in the bill, Lord Morpeth first gives a history of the principal stages of the various inquiries and commissions which had been helped on by all parties, and by successive Governments. He states that he has nothing new to bring forward, and can but repeat the information gained by others. He goes on to show by elaborate statistics the waste of life in large towns.

" Thus the inhabitants of London," he sums up, " compared with England at large, lose eight years of their lives, of Liverpool nineteen. The population of the large towns in England being 4,000,000, the annual loss is between 21,000 and 22,000." [1]

But all places are not equally unhealthy, as further statistics strikingly show. Where do we find the greatest number of deaths ? Is it where wages are lowest and the people poorest ? What did Lord Morpeth tell the House ?

" Let it not be said," he urges, " that the greater rate of mortality in certain districts is owing to extreme poverty and the want of the

[1] Lord Morpeth speaks here of the saving of life in large towns only.

necessaries of life. The condition of the labourers
of the west, the lowness of their wages and the
consequent scantiness of their food and clothing,
have been the subject of public animadversion.
The mortality of the south-western district, which
includes Cornwall, Devon, Somerset, Dorset, and
Wilts, is only 1 in 52—not 2 per cent; while that
of the north - western, including Cheshire and
Lancashire, is 1 in 37. With the exception of
the Cornish miners the condition of labourers
throughout the western counties is nearly the
same, yet in Wiltshire, the county of lowest
wages, the deaths are 1 in 49, in Lancashire
1 in 36. The average age at death in Wiltshire
was thirty-five, in Lancashire twenty-two. The
Wiltshire labourer's average age was thirty-five,
that of the Liverpool operative fifteen. At Manchester, in 1836, the average consumption per head
of the population was 105 lb. of butcher's meat
—about 2 lb. a-week (exclusive of bacon, pork,
fish, and poultry) ; the average age at death was
twenty years." He then brings forward evidence
of the preventibleness of most of the premature
deaths.

Having proved the extent of the evil, Lord

Morpeth proceeded to show how it was proposed to meet it,—by what machinery of central board, inspectors, &c; and, lastly, he entered into the money-saving that would be effected were thorough sanitary measures carried out. He cites Dr Playfair's estimates, which give the money loss, through unnecessary sickness and death, at £11,000,000 for England and Wales, and at £20,000,000 for the United Kingdom. This loss arises from many causes : the expenses of direct attendance on the sick ; the loss of what they would have earned ; the loss caused by the premature death of productive contributors to the national wealth ; and the expenses of premature funerals.

But the measure which was framed to relieve this sum of misery, though well and carefully prepared, was again to be thrown out!

It was weary work. The years were passing away, and nothing was being done. My grandfather used to come home saddened by each new defeat. He was sad at the delay, but he was not disheartened ; he knew that the thing would be done in time, and that the progress must be slow. He could wait calmly in that belief and enjoy fully the beauty of the sunset light during the summer evenings passed in our beautiful field, overlooking the green slopes and large trees of Caen Wood, Highgate. There our friends used to come to us, amongst others Professor Owen, Robert Browning, William and Mary Howitt, and Hans Christian Andersen; and we spent evenings that I can never forget, staying out constantly till the moon rose or the stars came out. How he loved nature and all happy things!

His faith did not err. The work of urging had not been in vain; the movement could not be stopped; the time was ripe.

The bill had been thrown out in 1847, but in 1848 the first sanitary law, the Public Health Act, passed!

CHAPTER VIII.

OFFICIAL LIFE—GENERAL BOARD OF HEALTH, 1848–1854.

IMMEDIATELY after the passing of the Public Health Act, Lord Morpeth wrote to my grandfather that the changes made in the bill during its passage through Parliament had prevented the creation of· any post which could be offered to him. Lord Morpeth said, however, that if Dr Southwood Smith would give the department the advantage both of his presence and counsel by accepting a seat on the Board, he hoped to provide for him a permanent post, by means of a supplementary Act, "The Diseases Prevention Act," which the Government expected to pass shortly. In answer to this my grandfather wrote as follows :—

38 FINSBURY SQUARE, *Sept.* 12, 1848.

MY DEAR LORD MORPETH,—I thank you very sincerely for your kind communication. . . . Thanks to your Lordship's indefatigable exertions, a position is now gained from which it is possible to attack, with some hope of success, the sources of excessive sickness and of premature mortality. You have at last laid the foundation of Practical Sanitary Improvement ; but the structure is still to be raised, and if, as your Lordship intimates, both you and the Government are desirous that I should assist you in this labour, no one will apply himself with a deeper feeling of responsibility, or with greater earnestness, to what her Majesty justly calls "this beneficent work."

Your Lordship will remember how earnest I was in December last, on the publication of the Bishop of London's Pastoral Letter, that we should at once avail ourselves of the power of the Contagious Diseases Act ; as well to make immediate preparation against the threatened visitation of cholera, as to check the progress of our own native epidemics, then and still so frightfully prevalent ; diseases manifestly dependent on conditions within our control, and highly favourable to the spread of the pestilence then menacing, and now still more nearly menacing us. The Bishop of London had called earnestly upon the clergymen of his diocese to co-operate with the medical profession in this object ; and being desirous of ascertaining the state of intelligence and feeling of this natural class of co-operators in such a work, I visited privately every clergyman in the Eastern District of London and discussed the subject with them.

Without a single exception, I found them impressed with a sense of the necessity of doing something, and with a conviction that they might materially help the medical profession in carrying out any plan of operation proposed by authority. The necessity of some such general plan is greater now than it was then, on account of the continual prevalence in their severest forms of our own epidemics, and of the nearer approach of cholera. The new " Contagious Diseases Act," the " Public Health Act," and the new " Metropolitan Sewers Act," taken together,

afford greater facilities for meeting this necessity than ever before existed ; and certainly it
is now in the power of the Government to do
more for securing the public health, and improving the physical condition of the population,
than has ever yet been attempted in any age
or nation,—a power which, if wisely and successfully exerted, will reflect the highest honour on
the Government and the country.

My intimate relation with the origin and progress of this work, and my deep conviction that
it is one of the most useful to which experience
and science can be applied, would render it a
satisfaction to me to spend the remainder of
my life in assisting to complete it.—I am, my
Lord, with much esteem and regard, very faithfully yours,   SOUTHWOOD SMITH.

The dates given at the head of this chapter
(1848 to 1854) cover the period when the
Sanitary cause was completely successful, and
when my grandfather found himself one of the
heads of a Government department devoted to
the furtherance of sanitary measures throughout
the kingdom—a department which was called the

General Board of Health. Here, at offices in
Whitehall, in daily conference with Lord Ashley
(afterwards the Earl of Shaftesbury) and Mr
Edwin Chadwick, he could propagate knowledge
on questions relating to the public health, and
carry out sanitary measures, as from a powerful
centre, having the authority of a Government
department.

This power of carrying out his convictions to
practical issues was an immense satisfaction to
my grandfather's mind, and many were the congratulations which he received on this public
appointment. The following, from a Portsmouth
physician, is interesting :—

October 8, 1848.

SIR,—Though personally a stranger, permit
me to offer my sincere congratulations on your
appointment by her Majesty's Government to the
Board of Health, where the talents you have so
long displayed will have scope for the full share
of utility.

I have traced and followed you in the various
publications issued by the Government and the
Health of Towns Association for several years
past, and having myself, though in a much more

confined area, mingled with public life, I know
the heart - burnings, the disappointments and
annoyances, to which in such a course a man is
necessarily exposed ; but if reward come at last—
though the delay has almost made the heart sick
—one is then amply repaid, especially in a case
like yours, when a whole kingdom will applaud
the appointment.

Permit me again, sir, to beg your acceptance
of my congratulations.—I am, sir, your obedient
servant,   —— ——

To Dr SOUTHWOOD SMITH, Whitehall.

Almost the first work which the Board of
Health had to do was to take measures to resist
an epidemic of Asiatic cholera. This it did by
sending down inspectors from London to instruct
and aid the local authorities in organising plans
for systematic cleansing, and for the removal of
the sick. The Board also issued " Notifications "
for the purpose of instructing the public as to
what precautions were necessary to avert an
attack. But above all, it organised, at my grandfather's instance, what was called the "system of
house-to-house visitation." My grandfather was

of opinion that in every instance an attack of cholera is preceded by a period of a few days (sometimes only of a few hours) of premonitory symptoms, which, since they are painless, escape notice; and that, unless a specially appointed medical visitor goes round to the houses of the less educated to inquire, and almost to cross-question, as to the existence of these symptoms, and to treat the disease *at once*, this stage rapidly passes on into developed cholera, when recovery becomes all but hopeless. These facts and experiences are brought out in the General Board of Health's Report on the Cholera Epidemic of 1848-49, presented to Parliament in 1850.

In relation to this, Lord Brougham thus wrote to my grandfather :—

" I also proclaimed [1] your important statement of the *preventive cure* of cholera, bearing further testimony to the soundness of your views from Sir J. Mordaunt's account given to me in the Malta case.

" I availed myself of the opportunity to give you just praise, and to note your many valuable

[1] In the House of Lords.

services to the country. Lord Lansdowne amply concurred in the statement by his cheers. But such things are never reported. Had you given a vote or an opinion on a contested party matter, all the papers would have chronicled your merits and our eulogies of you.—Ever yours truly,

"H. BROUGHAM."

Another of the subjects which the Board of Health took up was that of quarantine. Their first report on that subject, issued in 1850, was considered of sufficient importance to be translated into various foreign languages, and was ordered to be presented to the Parliaments of France and Italy. I think that, even if recent discoveries have modified some of the opinions there advanced, all the progress which has been made in the prevention of disease by quarantine regulations has been in the direction there indicated— that is, in plans for cleanliness, for the letting in of light and air, and for the isolation of infected persons in pure air, thus diluting the poison— rather than in plans for shutting them into confined quarters as was formerly done, thereby concentrating the poison.

The question of putting a stop to burials in overcrowded churchyards was also taken up by the Board. Their report on "A General Scheme for Extra-mural Sepulture" was published also in the same year (1850), and proved very clearly the evils arising from the crowded state of churchyards at that time.

The Board proposed that a Government department should be established which should be intrusted with the care of the whole question of the burial of the dead; that, in future, interment should take place only in ground remote from large towns; and that everything should be arranged decorously and reverently. My grandfather, personally, was much interested in adding an element of beauty in the form of exquisite and appropriate cemetery churches and chapels. But only the preventive part of the scheme was carried out. What was actually achieved was the closing of the overcrowded churchyards; the provision of other grounds has been left for private enterprise.

Thus, for six years, earnest men, at the head of a Health Department, spread information and gave advice. The newspapers of the period contained many notices of the various practical measures devised by this department, together with comments and leading articles on its reports on such large and pressing questions as cholera, quarantine, extra-mural sepulture, and water-supply. The newspapers, indeed, began to devote much space to the discussion of health questions in all forms, so that at last a widespread interest was aroused.

Then came a time when the chief question was, *not* as to the principles, but as to what machinery could best be employed to carry out those principles.

The fear of "centralisation," and the desire for local self-government, which is strong in the English people, caused opposition in Parliament to the continuance of any Government department having such large control over the expenditure of public money on local objects; so that in 1854 the original Board of Health ceased to exist, but did not cease till sanitary principles and sanitary science, once unknown or despised, were acknowledged throughout the country, and recognised as one of the fundamental needs lying at the root of all efforts to benefit the community.

With the ending of this department my grand-father's official life came to a close. From a personal point of view this cessation of his public work was somewhat softened by the following letter, written at the desire of the Prime Minister :—

WHITEHALL, 12*th August,* 1854.

SIR—I am directed by Viscount Palmerston to inform you that he cannot allow you to quit the Board which this day ceases to exist by the expiration of the Act of Parliament by which it was constituted, without conveying to you the full approbation of her Majesty's Government of the zealous, able, and indefatigable manner in which you have performed the important duties which have belonged to your official situation ; and his Lordship desires me to express to you the great regret which he feels, that an adverse decision of the House of Commons as to an arrangement which his Lordship had proposed for the re-construction of the Board of Health has led to so abrupt a cessation of your employment. —I am, sir, your obedient servant,

HENRY FITZROY.

Dr SOUTHWOOD SMITH.

According to the rules of the service, my grand-father was not entitled to a retiring allowance, because so much of the work he had done had been unpaid. A few years afterwards, however, a Government pension was awarded him in consideration of the services which he had rendered to the country.

CHAPTER IX.

RETIREMENT FROM PUBLIC LIFE—ST GEORGE'S
HILL, WEYBRIDGE, 1854–1860.

WHEN his official life came to a close, my grandfather retired to a house on Weybridge Heath,
and he met the sudden cessation of his eager
public life with the same calm courage with which
he had met all the other crises in his career.

This house had been built on a beautiful spot
as a gathering-place for his much-loved and somewhat scattered family, and the beauty of its position came to be a great comfort to him when he
turned his quiet days to the prosecution of literary
work in his little study, which, opening on to a
sunny terraced walk, overlooked, through vistas
of dark-green pines and yellow birch-trees,
the miles of blue distance which stretched out
southwards to the Surrey and Hampshire hills.

Through the kindness of Lord Ellesmere, whose property adjoined, there was a small private gate leading from our own little firwood on to St George's Hill itself; and, in the intervals of his writing, frequent strolls on to its beautiful slopes were a great source of pleasure during that first autumn and in all the ensuing years. The heather banks and wooded dells brought him much joy ; for, as always, it was in the presence of nature and in the stillness of the country that he gathered strength. The strain of the last few months had been great, and it was well that the closing of the year brought with it the much-needed rest.

He now gave a good deal of time to physiological study, turning to his old subjects with the vigour of a younger man, and entering with the deepest interest into the discoveries of later science. He did this with a view of bringing his early book, ' The Philosophy of Health,' which at the time of its publication had made so much mark, up to the standard of modern knowledge ; and though he did not live to complete this task, the reading for it gave a living interest to those years of quiet country life.

He had also much satisfaction in writing and

publishing a pamphlet called 'Results of Sanitary Improvement,' based mainly on the experience obtained in the " Model Dwellings " for the working classes, of which he had been the originator. This pamphlet, coming as it did before many influential men throughout the country, spread the good news of progress far and wide.

A further instance of the fruit of his labours was afforded him by his visit to Edinburgh, in November 1855, when he lectured on his own subject, " Epidemics," at the Philosophical Institution, where a brilliant reception and distinguished audience awaited him.[1]

I have a vivid recollection of his pleasure in the beauty of Alnwick as we journeyed north — of its old castle's warm grey walls, its lovely woods and clear running streams, during a sunny Sunday which we passed there,— the gold and russet tints of autumn shining out against a perfectly blue sky ; and I also remember the satisfaction he had in hearing from the Mayor, who took us round the town,

[1] Epidemics considered with relation to their Common Nature and to Climate and Civilisation. Published by Edmonston & Douglas, Edinburgh, 1856.

of the pure water and good drainage lately introduced. Alnwick was, I believe, one of the first places which adopted the sanitary measures advised by the General Board of Health, so that here he had the gratification of seeing some of the great reforms practically carried out.

As I am recalling the various sources of comfort which came to my grandfather during these years at Weybridge, I must mention the great happiness which arose from the opening out of the lives of two of his granddaughters, Miranda and Octavia Hill; for it was at this time that they—at the ages of nineteen and sixteen —took the responsibilities of their lives upon themselves, and began the great and good works which they have since carried to such wide issues.

In his retirement, letters of appreciation and sympathy reached him from many of the public men with whom he had worked, expressing in various ways that which Lord Shaftesbury, who knew him as well as any, gives as his own feeling when writing to a mutual friend :—

" I have known Dr Southwood Smith well, having sat with him during four years and in very trying times at the Board of Health. A more able, diligent, zealous, and benevolent man does not exist. No work ever seemed too much for him if it were to do good. His great services will not, I fear, be appreciated in this generation."

Such words as these cannot but have been gratifying to my grandfather; but in 1858 those who shared these sentiments resolved to make a clearer and more public demonstration of their sense of the value of the services which he had rendered to the country. At a preliminary meeting held on the 7th May 1856 it was agreed that this recognition should take the form, primarily, of a memorial bust, to be presented to a suitable public institution. This intention was communicated to Dr Southwood Smith at the final meeting held at the house of Lord Shaftesbury, 24 Grosvenor Square, on the 6th of December 1858, and was accompanied by a short address.

I give his own words of thanks, as they show not only the pleasure this recognition afforded him, but also — what is so characteristic of him —his joy in the progress of his cause, quite apart from his personal share in it :—

"My Lord, I need not say how deeply I feel the kindness that prompted the proceeding which has led to this meeting. If anything could increase the intensity of that feeling, it would be the words in which you have given expression to your sentiments in this matter, and to those of the rest of the subscribers to this recognition.

"The labourers in the work of sanitary reform have been many; and it is by the united efforts of some of the most enlightened, disinterested, and learned men that shed lustre on this century, that this great work has been placed in its present position.

"That such names as those which grace this Tablet[1] should have united to express their sense of the value of any part which I may have taken in this work, will ever be to me a source, I do not say of happiness only, but of that rare and pure happiness which results not alone from the inward consciousness of devotion to duty through encouragement and discouragement, through evil and through good report, but also from the knowledge that such judges of the matter justify that consciousness,

[1] See Appendix II., p. 164.

and in my own individual case have so placed
their judgment on record, that it may be present
to me to the latest day of my life and to my
children and my children's children.

" I will only add that the honourable names
on this Record give me this further delight,
that they are to me a pledge that Sanitary
Improvement will go on. They thus bear their
testimony to their sense of its importance, and
they, from their position and character, can
ensure its progress. The first labourers in this
work may not be permitted to complete it,—
they seldom are in any great work ; but, who-
ever may have the satisfaction of completing
it, that work — whatever obstacles may retard,
whatever short - sighted and short - lived interests may oppose it, however it may seem for
a while not to advance — *that work will be
done ;* and the time will come when not only
the professional man and the educator, but the
legislator, the statesman, the general, the minister of religion—in a word, every one to whom
is entrusted the care, the guidance, and the
control of numbers, will feel ashamed to be
ignorant, and indeed will be accounted unfit

K

for his office if he be ignorant, of the laws
of human health and life."

.   .   .   .

Yes! That his work had lived and would
live, this was what he cared for. This it was
that kept him uniformly brave and bright, and
made him say to me one evening in tones of
grateful joy—we were sitting on the wide balcony
watching the moon rise over the fir-tree tops,
his hand in mine as of old,—

"I have indeed succeeded! I have lived
to see seven millions of the public money expended on this great cause. If any one had
told me, when I began, that this would be,
I should have considered it absolutely in-
credible."

CHAPTER X.

THE SUNSET OF LIFE—ITALY, 1861.

My grandfather had travelled abroad but little during his strenuous life. He had, it is true, been to Paris in 1850, accompanied by Mr Charles Macaulay, Dr John Sutherland, and Mr (afterwards Sir Henry) Rawlinson, on business connected with the General Board of Health scheme for extra-mural sepulture, but, except on that occasion, he had not left England.

So that when in 1857 he was asked to join a party of three proceeding to Milan for the purpose of examining the irrigation works of that city, he gladly undertook the journey, which was to lead them *viâ* Marseilles and along the Cornice Road, then traversed by carriage only. The beauty of Italy thus came before him with full freshness at the age of seventy, and he returned strengthened and invigorated.

The following year my grandfather lost his wife. She died at The Pines, at Weybridge, after a short illness, in the summer of 1858.

Two years later he was able to carry out his cherished hope of returning to Italy, and we went to Florence, where his daughter Emily had been living for some years. She welcomed us to the rooms she had secured in an old palace beyond the Arno — to the artistic Italian surroundings of which she had added something of the atmosphere of an English home.

His delight in the art and nature of Florence and its environs was intense, and the beauty of land and sky seems to make a fitting setting for the end of such a life as his.

He stood on the old jeweller's bridge, one autumn evening late in November, and watched the sun go down behind the western hill of the rushing Arno; and the sunset of his own life came soon after. Perhaps he had lingered too long gazing at this beautiful scene; for a chill, producing rapid bronchitis, took him from us on the 10th December 1861.

Towards the end, when he knew he was passing away, after other gentle loving words, almost his last were—with a sweet triumphant smile—

" Draw up the blind and let me see the stars ;
for I still love the beauty."

At the cemetery at Porta Pinti are some
sombre gates with, over them, the words " Ils
se reposent de leurs travaux, et leurs œuvres les
suivent." Those black gates opened one sunny
December morning and showed a sloping avenue
of marble tombs, tangles of pink and of white
China roses in full flower falling over them, and
at the end a tall white cross shining in the
sunlight against the blue Italian sky,—fit type
of the black gates of death, which had rolled
back to let him pass into the Eternal Light
beyond.

There we left him in completest trust, our
" Knight Errant," after his life's warfare.

For there is a poem by Adelaide Procter (on
whom written I know not) which seems to give,
with the full force of poetical presentation, the
spirit of the Life I have tried to depict. It even
seems to follow the very order of the periods
of that life — *our* hero following the course of

hers; and thus fulfilling Mrs Browning's words
when she says—

> "Ingemisco, ingemisco!
> Is ever a lament begun
> By any mourner under sun
> Which, ere it endeth, suits but one?"

In my extract-book the following lines have
lain away for the nearly forty years which have
passed since he went from us, and they still
remain, to me, the best expression of what he
was. I find, in pencil, against the verses the
place or date which they symbolise.

If those who have read these pages see their
aptness, they will learn from them, more than
from any words of mine, what measure of man
he was.

A KNIGHT ERRANT.

> "Though he lived and died amongst us,   *Bristol,*
>   Yet his name may be enrolled   *Edinburgh,*
> With the knights whose deeds of daring   *Yeovil.*
>   Ancient chronicles have told.

> Still a stripling he encountered
>   Poverty, and suffered long,
> Gathering force from every effort
>   Till he knew his arm was strong.

Then his heart and life he offered
  To his radiant mistress—Truth.
Never thought or dream of faltering
  Marred the promise of his youth.

So he rode forth to defend her,   *London,* 1820
  And her peerless worth proclaim ;   *to* 1854.
Challenging each recreant doubter
  Who aspersed her spotless name.

First upon his path stood *Ignorance,*
  Hideous in his brutal might ;
Hard the blows and long the battle
  Ere the monster took to flight.

Then, with light and fearless spirit,
  Prejudice he dared to brave,
Hunting back the lying craven
  To her black sulphureous cave.

Followed by his servile minions,
  Custom, the old Giant, rose ;
Yet he, too, at last was conquered
  By the good Knight's weighty blows.

Once again he rose a conqueror,   *Weybridge.*
  And, though wounded in the fight,
With a dying smile of triumph
  Saw that Truth had gained her right.

On his failing ear re-echoing
  Came the shouting round her throne ;
Little cared he that no future
  With her name would link his own.

Spent with many a hard-fought battle
  Slowly ebbed his life away,
And the crowd that flocked to greet her
  Trampled on him where he lay.

Gathering all his strength he saw her   *Italy.*
  Crowned and reigning in her pride,
Looked his last upon her beauty,
  Raised his eyes to God—and died."

—A. A. PROCTER.

VIEW FROM PORTA PINTI.

CHAPTER XI.

THE AFTERGLOW.

It was at this time that the Prince Consort died, and England was full of mourning. Lord Shaftesbury speaks, in his diary of December 16, 1861, of that national loss, and then alludes to the death of my grandfather in these words :—

"I hear, too, that my valued friend and co-adjutor in efforts for the sanitary improvement of England is gone—the learned, warm-hearted, highly-gifted Southwood Smith."

But the work he had set on foot and the principles he had established did not end with his life. They have gone on with an ever-increasing vitality to this day.

The efforts he made for the non-employment of women and young children in mines have resulted in the entire cessation of the practice ;

while his work for the provision of proper
schooling for factory children has culminated
now in a whole system of workhouse and factory supervision and in the school-board system
throughout the land. Intramural burial is virtually at an end. And
the "Home Hospitals" and "Nursing Homes,"
which are established in all our large towns, are
the successors of that "Sanatorium, or Home
in Sickness," which he devised, and for which
Charles Dickens pleaded in its early days.

The marshy Bethnal Green and Spitalfields,
where he first visited the individual homes,
and which he took Lord Normanby and Lord
Ashley to see, are now comparatively healthy
places. He found them without water; there
is now water laid on to every house. He found
them without drainage; now a complete and
scientific system of drainage exists throughout
the metropolis. The "£7,000,000 of public
money spent on sanitary reform," over which
he rejoiced so greatly, is, since he spoke in 1857,
increased by all the millions spent on such works
in the last forty years.

His first set of "Model Dwellings," in the

St Pancras Road, is now multiplied by the
countless blocks of such in all the large towns
of England. Sanitary Law and Sanitary Inspection everywhere prevail, and the thousands
of lives annually saved—the lowered death-rate
both in town and country — attests the power
of the laws he was one of the first to perceive
and proclaim.

To show the saving of life in London alone,
the death-rate in the early "forties" was 26 in
the thousand, it is now 19; whilst in the Model
Dwellings the improvement is even more striking, since there it is not more than half that of
London at large. To show how completely the
experiment he made to prove the possible health-
fulness of such dwellings has answered, it is only
necessary to quote the figures given in the report just issued for this fifty-third year of the
Society which he founded.

"The rate of mortality," we learn, "in the
Dwellings of the Association, was 9'64 per 1000,
including 12 deaths which occurred in hospitals,
infirmaries, &c. In the entire metropolis the
rate was 18'2 per 1000. As regards infant mortality, the deaths under one year of age were

at the rate of 79 in every 1000 births; and in the entire metropolis, at the rate of 161 per 1000 births."

Allusion has been made to the bust which was executed as a tribute to the public services of my grandfather by those whom we have called the Pioneers of Sanitary Reform — Lord Normanby, Lord Shaftesbury, Lord Carlisle (formerly Lord Morpeth), Charles Dickens, Mr Slaney, and others. This bust is now in the National Portrait Gallery, and accompanying it are the following lines by Leigh Hunt, which proclaim the services of his life in the cause of the poor to wider circles still:—

> " Ages shall honour, in their hearts enshrined,
> Thee, Southwood Smith, Physician of Mankind;
> Bringer of Air, Light, Health into the Home
> Of the rich Poor of happier times to come!"

APPENDIX

APPENDIX I.

LETTER FROM MR TAYLOR, ASSISTANT RETURNING OFFICER OF THE WHITECHAPEL UNION, TO DR SOUTHWOOD SMITH; written at the request of the latter, for Lord Ashley's use, after their personal inspection of Bethnal Green and Whitechapel.

289 BETHNAL GREEN ROAD, *Feb.* 5, 1842.

MY DEAR DOCTOR,—Lord Ashley, the Honble. Mr Ashley, and yourself visited the following places with me. I have arranged them in the form of a table: in one column is the name of the street, and, opposite, a brief notice of its condition, with an occasional remark by which his Lordship may recognise it.

Apologising for the length of time that has elapsed since I promised to forward this account to you, I remain, dear Doctor, Your Obed^nt. Servt,

T. TAYLOR.

First Visit.

Back of Chester Place.	Open ditch and several pigsties.
Pitt Street.	A wretched road, no drainage. Hon. Mr Ashley spoke to one of the inhabitants respecting the state of the road.
Burnham Square.	Houses built on undrained ground.
Grosvenor Street.	Undrained houses on one side not supplied with water (all the houses on this estate, to the amount of about 200 or more, in the same condition, the inhabitants having to go to a distant pump or beg of their neighbours, who have had it laid on at their own expense, and who for giving it are liable to punishment). Bonner Street has an open ditch in front of part of it.
Bonner Street.	
Pleasant Place.	Road a perfect quagmire.
Green Street.	Stagnant water on southern side and also on part of the northern.
Baker Street.	Houses back to back, consisting of two rooms, each one above the other. Privies close to windows of lower rooms. Baker's night-yard is in this street.
Digby Street.	
James Street.	Another night-yard.
Bethnal Green Road (eastern end).	No drainage, many of the houses having 10 inches to 2 feet of water in the cellars, which are from 3 feet to 3 feet 8 inches only below the level of the road.
Sanderson's Gardens.	Houses on each side below the level of the pathway, which has a gutter in the middle. (Lord Ashley spoke to one of the inhabitants of this place.)
Pitt Street, Bethnal Green Road.	A narrow street with only surface drainage. (Fever was very prevalent here.)

Cambden Gardens.	Houses built on the soil, many of them not being larger than an 8-feet cube, are inhabited.
Lamb's Fields.	An acre at least of complete marsh and three open ditches—one on the north, another in the middle, and the third to the eastern side close to the backs of the houses in North Street.
London Street.	Undrained.
Rupia Lane.	Two open ditches.
Ann's Place.	Open sewer in front of some of the houses.
Houses at the back of Ann's Place.	The open sewer from Ann's Place passes beneath one of the houses and then is again open to the houses at the back, but is boarded in so that Lord Ashley had to mount a boundary stone to obtain the view of it.
A group of streets to the north of Slacky Road.	All the houses stained with damp to a height varying from 1 to 2 or more feet.
Warmer Place.	An open sewer in front of the houses giving off bubbles of gas very freely.
Wellington Pond.	A large piece of water into which the above sewer drains — gives off constantly innumerable bubbles of gas, and the stench is sometimes abominable. Persons who have accidentally fallen into it, though taken out immediately, have all died.
A thoroughfare leading from bottom of Pollards Row to Wellington Row.	The lucifer match manufactory faces this road, into which we all went. An open ditch in the most filthy condition.
Squirries Street.	Green stagnant water on each side.
Wellington Row.	Lower rooms all damp. An open ditch in front. Western end soft mud, into which the wheels of a waggon sank 14 or 15 inches as it passed.

L

North Street and some of the houses at the back. — Lord Ashley saw the landlord of some of them.

Waterloo Town (several streets). — All undrained, but part of Manchester Street and Albion Street. Many variations of level of several feet at a distance of a few yards only, as Manchester Place, Derbyshire Street, Sale Street. Many of the houses back to back and consisting of five ground-floor rooms only.

Second Visit.

George Street. — A centre gutter full of stagnant water.

Old Bethnal Green Road. — Has had a sewer made recently, but houses do not communicate with it.

Clare Street, Felix Street, Centre Street, Cambridge Circus, Minerva Street, Matilda Street, Hope Street, Temple Street, Charles Street, Charlotte Street, Durham Street. — All built on undrained ground, and the houses affected with damp.

Court opposite to Cambridge Road. — One privy to several houses, and mosses growing on the damp brick of the houses to the height of 4 or 5 feet from the ground.

Nova Scotia Gardens. — Several feet below the road in many parts, the drainage of which it receives. (Here lived the burkers of the Italian boy.)

Virginia Row, York Street, and the streets to the east. — Undrained, having stagnant water in them.

Rose Court. — Most wretched hovels.

Typen Street — (Where the child was burnt.)

Satchwell Rents.	The privies form part of the ground-floor of these houses. Lord Ashley inspected the first house ; *no* yards.
Mount Street.	Level of the houses very uneven ; many below the level of the road. The un-drained portion of this street suffered from fever to an awful extent, while the high and drained part had scarcely a case.
Courts out of Mount Street.	Dung-heap in one. Lord Ashley saw the landlord of another and spoke to him.
Collingwood Street.	Houses on one side much lower than on the other ; very badly drained, and not a healthy-looking person or child in the street.

APPENDIX II.

RECOGNITION OF THE PUBLIC SERVICES OF
DR SOUTHWOOD SMITH.

At a Meeting held at the residence of the Earl of
Shaftesbury on the 7th of May 1856

IT WAS RESOLVED

That this Meeting, deeply impressed with the
untiring and successful labours of Dr Southwood Smith
in the cause of social amelioration, and specially recog-
nising the value of these labours in the great cause of

SANITARY IMPROVEMENT,

are anxious to tender him some mark of their personal
esteem. That accordingly a bust of Dr Southwood
Smith be executed in marble, and presented to some
suitable institution, as an enduring memorial of his
eminent services in the promotion of the Public Health.

The following is a List of the Subscribers :—

Viscount Palmerston, K.G., G.C.B., First Lord of the Treasury.

The Earl of Carlisle, K.G., Lord Lieutenant of Ireland.

The Earl of Harrowby, Chancellor of the Duchy of Lancaster.

The Marquis of Lansdowne, K.G.

The Marquis of Normanby, K.G., G.C.B., Ambassador at Florence.

The Right Honourable W. F. Cowper, M.P., President of the Board of Health.

Thomas Graham, Esq., F.R.S., Master of the Mint.

The Duke of Buccleuch.

The Duke of Newcastle.

The Earl of Ellesmere.

The Earl Fortescue, K.G.

The Earl of St Germans.

The Earl of Harrington.

The Earl of Shaftesbury.

The Lord Bishop of London.

The Lord Bishop of St Asaph.

The Lord Bishop of Ripon..

The Lord Brougham and Vaux.

The Viscount Ebrington, M.P.

The Viscount Goderich, M.P.

The Lord Robert Grosvenor, M.P.

The Lord Claude Hamilton, M.P.

The Lord Stanley of Bickerstaffe, M.P.

The Honourable A. Kinnaird, M.P.

Sir Edward Borough, Bart.

Sir E. N. Buxton, Bart.

The Rev. Sir H. Dukinfield, Bart.

Sir John Easthope, Bart.

Sir Ralph Howard, Bart.

Sir Samuel Morton Peto, Bart.

Sir John Ramsden, Bart.

Sir Erskine Perry, Q.C., M.P.

The Lord Mayor.

The Dean of Ely.

Henry Austin, Esq.

B. G. Babington, Esq., M.D.

Thomas Baker, Esq.

Joseph Bateman, Esq., LL.D.

John Batten, Esq.

G. Beaman, Esq., M.D.

Thomas Bell, Esq., F.R.S.

Joseph Brotherton, Esq., M.P.

Alexander Browne, Esq., M.D.

A. Collyer, Esq.

The Rev. J. Cumming, D.D.

The Rev. R. S. Daniell, M.A.

Charles Dickens, Esq.

John Dillon, Esq.

William Farr, Esq., M.D.

Arthur Farre, Esq., M.D.

John Finlaison, Esq.

C. Gatliff, Esq.

F. D. Goldsmid, Esq.

R. D. Grainger, Esq., F.R.S.

Samuel Gurney, Esq.

J. F. Hart, Esq.

A. Hassall, Esq., M.D.

James Heywood, Esq., M.P.

Rowland Hill, Esq.
M. D. Hill, Esq., Q.C.
F. Hill, Esq.
A. Hill, Esq.
E. Hill, Esq.
Gurney Hoare, Esq.
P. H. Holland, Esq.
T. Jones Howell, Esq.
The Rev. Charles Hume, M.A.
R. W. Kennard, Esq.
Duncan M'Laren, Esq.
J. Leslie, Esq.
Waller   Lewis,   Esq.,   M.B.,
F.G.S.
C. Z. Macaulay, Esq.
J. J. Mechi, Esq.
R. Monckton Milnes, Esq., M.P.

Gavin Milroy, Esq., M.D.
James Morrison, Esq.
Professor Owen, F.R.S.
Tucker Radford, Esq., M.D.
Robert Rawlinson, Esq.
J. A. Roebuck, Esq., M.P.
W. Rogers, Esq.
S. S. Scriven, Esq.
R. A. Slaney, Esq., M.P.
J. J. Smith Esq.
James Startin, Esq.
John Sutherland, Esq., M.D.
Thomas Thornely, Esq., M.P.
John Thwaites, Esq.
J. W. Tottie, Esq.
Thomas Tooke, Esq., F.R.S.
E. Westall, Esq.[1]

[1] It will be seen that a very large number of the names on this list are those of men who had personally worked with my grandfather or had watched and helped as labourers in the Sanitary cause from the beginning.—G. L.

INDEX.

PRINTED BY WILLIAM BLACKWOOD AND SONS.

For EU product safety concerns, contact us at Calle de José Abascal, 56–1°,
28003 Madrid, Spain or eugpsr@cambridge.org.